Educational Psychology

Educational Psychology

Experimentation in Problems and Methods in Teaching

L.N. Verma

RAWAT PUBLICATIONS
Jaipur • New Delhi • Bangalore • Hyderabad • Guwahati • Kolkata

ISBN 978-81-316-0581-3

Published by
Prem Rawat for **Rawat Publications**
Satyam Apts, Sector 3, Jawahar Nagar, Jaipur 302 004 (India)
Phone: 0141 265 1748/7006 Fax: 0141 265 1748
E-mail: info@rawatbooks.com
Website: www.rawatbooks.com

New Delhi Office
4858/24, Ansari Road, Daryaganj, New Delhi 110 002
Phone: 011 2326 3290

Also at *Bangalore, Hyderabad, Guwahati* and *Kolkata*

Typeset by Rawat Computers, Jaipur
Printed at Nice Printing Press, New Delhi

Contents

Preface

The present work is designed to fulfil the needs of newly-trained teachers who have come out of the educational training institutions to enter the school classroom and face the pupils during the process of teaching.

In fact, most of the teachers do not know how to apply the educational and psychological principles they have learnt during the training. They enter the class, deliver the lecture, ask questions to answer and come out after the scheduled time. Is this teaching or telling?

The modern system of education is the process of development and behavioural change among the learners for social good. It is the preparation for life, and goes incessantly from infancy to maturity. In brief, the system and modern concept of teaching children in schools aims to develop their inherent capacities so that they may adapt to various situations during their life-long journey. It is the behavioural development and capacity to acquire skills for wholesome adjustment to various environmental situations – physical, social, economic and cultural.

This book aims to refresh teachers and to remind them of their job in the classroom. They should know their pupils' needs, interests and aptitude. The application of the principles of psychology is based on John Adams' motto: 'know the child before you teach him Latin'. Therefore, a teacher must find time to understand the pupils whom he or she is supposed to teach. The various parts of the book have been designed to meet the major objectives of teaching in the classroom. The author stresses on new approaches and aims to make the teachers learn their application in the classroom.

The teacher should try, as far as possible, to provide opportunities for interaction in the classroom. He/she may be integrative or dominative. An integrative teacher loves students and allows participation in the teaching work. He/she accepts, supports and further classifies the students' point of view and feelings. Thus, interaction may build a congenial classroom climate. The process of teaching may become a joy and pleasure both for the pupils and the teacher.

The author extends his gratitude to all those who have helped in the writing of this book. He is grateful to his teachers of education at Dayalbagh, Agra, for motivation and providing guidance during the preparation of the book.

The author is also deeply indebted to the publishers for their cooperation. The readers, scholars of education and pupils are the best judge and their suggestions and opinions are welcome.

L.N. Verma

Introduction

The book has five parts as under:

(i) Principles of Teaching Psychology and Inherent Powers of a Child
(ii) Process of Human Growth and Development
(iii) Learning, Motives and Individual Differences
(iv) Exceptional Children and Classroom Teaching
(v) Classroom, Social Learning and Teacher's Adjustment

Part I has three chapters: (i) Basic Principles of Teaching Process; (ii) Psychological Process of Learning: Methods and Scope; and (iii) Inherent Powers of a Child. These jointly become a part of educational psychology.

Teachers can solve their problems in the classroom by following the basic principles of educational psychology. The psychological process improves the methods of teaching. This includes primarily the factors such as understanding oneself and understanding the child.

A teacher must evaluate his or her capacities before he or she undertakes the noble profession of teaching. He/she should be aware of his/her ability to face different types of pupils, their background and their inherent powers. Teaching is not a profession which can be successfully carried out by just anyone. It requires academic knowledge as well as the skill to understand the pupils, their family background and environment. It is also essential for a teacher to know not only his/her own nature, mental and intellectual level, ultimate goal, philosophy of life and social relations but also of his/her colleagues. He/she should be careful about his/her behaviour towards pupils, their likes and dislikes, mode of interaction, etc. This helps them to become a good teacher. John Adams believed that for a teacher, it is more important to know the psychology of children than to be an expert academically.

The principles of psychology also help the teacher in the classroom to diagnose and solve problems that arise. Some of the problems which are faced by the teacher during teaching are:

(a) Backward child and to bring him/her at level with the other classmates
(b) Treatment essential for maladjusted children
(c) Maintaining discipline in the class
(d) Using methods to bring a physically or mentally-deformed child to the normal level of the class
(e) Using methods to create traits of self-study in pupils or the technique of self-motivation
(f) Dealing with delinquent children – means of sublimation or prevention

A teacher should constantly analyse his/her own methods of teaching, and try to revise them according to attitude, aptitude, interest and family background as well as the environment of children. The performance of a successful teacher invariably needs a thorough knowledge of educational psychology.

***

Pupils in a classroom differ very much. Personal traits of students are not one and the same. Their differences need careful adjustment for making them learn through the process of teaching.

The teacher should take into consideration the various aspects of his pupils such as variability, conformity and difference in the rate of learning and development. Pupils exhibit differences in physical and mental development, sociability, nature, rate of learning, ability, interest, etc.

Knowledge of human growth and development is essential for a teacher to study the nature of pupils' personality. It depends upon the fundamentals of psychology.

The process of human growth and development includes various aspects like physical, mental, emotional, moral, aesthetic and social, etc. Educational psychology studies all these aspects during various stages. The development process is the subject matter of the five chapters included in the second part. A teacher is required to follow the principles involved to bring home his pupils according to the objectives and norms desired for the change of their behaviour for the social good.

***

Learning and individual differences are present in all human beings. Our varying needs also make us different from each other. These differences compel each of us to behave differently. Each of us behaves differently in meeting his/her needs and also in solving his/her daily problems. Our behaviour is generally guided by our level of learning to deal with our problems. Different motives guide our actions.

The motives play a vital role in our varied actions and behaviour to a given problem and to meet our different needs. A motive is actually an urge which compels us to act and initiate in a particular direction. It comprises both our internal and external forces to act and face the problem. Psychologically, motive includes only those factors which cognitively control our actions. An individual, being different cognitively, acts differently.

In the third part, which contains four chapters, the levels of learning or our standards of cognition and their impact on our behaviour are discussed. This part also includes a discussion on learning and motivation, their various aspects, the process in the classroom, various concepts and also the nature of our training and its transference to deal with various subjects.

***

Part IV has again four chapters in all, dealing with exceptional children, including talented and gifted children, mentally challenged children, handicapped and delinquent children. A teacher in his/her classroom has to face several types of pupils. Some are bright, many slow and of average ability and a few who are dull. His/her task is to bring them all into a general process of teaching in a way that each of them displays some sort of progress in the course of learning.

The problem is that a few students who lag behind show diffident tendency in learning. They require special care by the teacher to bring them at par with the category of normal pupils. This is not an easy task and teachers generally overlook this responsibility. It creates problems and there are cases of pupils falling behind and unable to adjust with class activities. They are known as problem children and their behaviour reflects some sort of abnormality in the form of habits like apathy towards their class-mates, and often shows truancy and idleness, indiscipline and short temper. The teacher's problem becomes acute when such children demonstrate an anti-social behaviour, which proves harmful to both the teacher and classmates.

The problem of mentally challenged and delinquent children must be carefully dealt with by trained and experienced teachers of high moral character. This can be handled by a creative teacher better than others. A creative teacher possesses an ability to discover new solutions for a given problem or to produce new ideas and works of art to satisfy the needs of the delinquents. They should be kept under observation for sometime and given play therapy.

Gifted children generally possess the level of IQ ranging between 120 and 130 and above. They also create problems in the class and, sometimes, for the management of the school. They should be treated by providing opportunities to display their skills through activities like art, music, dramatics and scouting, NCC, hiking, tours and travels, etc. They should be provided their due status and positions in seminars and meetings. These activities may make them favourably adjusted with the school and classroom situations.

The teaching process in the classroom should include the paraphernalia to deal with all types of pupils, i.e., talented, average and backward or delinquent. The methodology of teaching should also be well-planned and supported by life experiences, including motivations to satisfy various categories of intelligent pupils.

***

The fifth and final part of the book presents an overview of classroom, social learning and teacher's adjustment. It has five chapters. The first social situation which a pupil encounters is his/her classroom. In the classroom, there are a number of situations which operate and influence pupils' attitude, ideas and behaviour. It is a theatre where pupils' performances are evaluated. It is here that the pupil remains alert to complete his task well and learn satisfactorily.

In a classroom, there are a number of students who interact with a learning situation during the course of teaching. The teaching process involves the entire group of learners. The teacher utilizes the capacities of the group of learners for making his/her teaching more effective. He/she remains alert to accommodate individual needs and the process generates a democratic atmosphere in the classroom, where the teacher teaches all and in the context of an individual's problems.

The teacher has also to face the classroom environment as a leader to maintain discipline. The quality of the teacher makes for quality education. A teacher can mould the behaviour of children in the desired manner only when he/she himself possesses a balanced personality, with good mental health.

Thus, focusing on the major aspects of educational psychology, this book will be of immense interest to educational planners, psychologists and policy makers.

Part I

Principles of Teaching Psychology and Inherent Powers of a Child

1

Basic Principles of Teaching Process

Classroom teaching and motivating pupils to learn cognitively are skills which a teacher should develop. It is not a routine activity of pouring facts about phenomena into the ears of students. It is a scientific process which prepares the pupils to learn with understanding and fulfil their objectives in view. The entire process is based on certain concepts of psychology. The teacher makes use of children's psychology of thinking, grasping the ideas and analysing their outcome. All efforts of the teacher should be directed towards making the process of learning effective and efficient. The basic principles of the teaching process are discussed in this chapter.

Know the Child

The learning skill is based on the knowledge of the subject or child. It is not an easy task but a crucial problem which is dealt through the psychology of a child. It is based on the principle of knowing children's attitude, interests, and above all, their behaviour towards the classroom activities. J.S. Ross, who is the well-known author of 'Educational Psychology', wrote: 'Know John before you teach him Latin' (Adams). This means that knowledge of any discipline can be imparted by understanding the behaviour of the learner. Teaching methodology for a novice is based on the skill to guide children. A teacher must be aware of pupils' interests, their attitude, behaviour and likes-dislikes. Beyond the character imbibed due to family and heredity, and also the environmental impact of neighbourhood and school, the teacher should know the pupils' physical make-up and mental attitude. Mental attitude includes power of memory, reasoning and judgement, attention span, imagination, moral values and understanding. These form the basic psychological principles to know the child before you start giving him/her material like facts, figures and instructions.

Educational psychology is not a new branch of knowledge. Aristotle, the Greek philosopher, is known for giving rigorous training to Alexander. In modern times, Europe-based educational psychologists' contributions are remembered by teachers to this day. They are J.S. Ross, J.H. Pestalozzi, J.F. Herbart and F.W. August Froebel. Later on, applied educational psychology became the cornerstone with the efforts and research of Charles Judd and Thorndike. They contributed and made the methods of education scientific. Thus, the field of educational psychology and its scope has gradually expanded over the last several decades.

In the Indian context, the development of educational psychology followed a different trend, as evident from the river valley civilization of more than 5,000 years. Contemporary society has its base in art, music, mathematics and astronomy. Altekar opines that ancient literature supports the fact that education was based on high ideals and self-realization. Its basic premise: the restless mind can be brought under control by ceaselessly striving through the practice of meditation.

Know Psychology

Education in India has made rapid progress since the 1950s and its psychological bearing is related to learning, readiness for learning, social adjustment and mental health.

The main aim of educational psychology is to study the child's behaviour and to modify it for the social good. It studies those processes which provide ways and means to bring under control the child's behaviour so that it might prove useful to society.

What is happening in schools these days? The child is made to memorize facts. The evaluation is based on the repetition of the memorized facts. Education has gone far away from the motives of social good and is not based on the child's interests.

Social Motives

The modern concept of education is to train the child from infancy to adulthood. It is the continuous process which makes children to be useful for society during their various stages of life. What do we derive from the above concept? Educational psychology is an applied knowledge which is based on laws of human behaviour. The laws of human behaviour are related to the social process.

Summing up the meaning of educational psychology, it can be concluded that it is the science of applying the principles of psychology concerned with human behaviour which might bring changes for adjustment to various problems of life and be proven good for society. As C.H. Judd defines: "It is the science which describes and explains the changes that take place in individuals as they pass through various stages of development from birth to maturity." By development, we mean the learning experiences of an individual, right from infancy to maturity. Human psychology becomes educational since it has contributed to the various conditions of life responsible for determination of learning, and also to prepare man to be fit for making adjustment to his family, society and nation.

Change of Personality

The general aim of educational psychology is to mould the complete personality of the child for the good. It motivates the child to adapt to various life situations so that he/she may become a useful unit of society and actively understand the continually changing world. Besides this, the educational psychological point of view also motivates the teacher to revise and remodel methods of teaching, making it creative and innovative in nature.

Skinner has advocated that there are certain specific aims of educational psychology in relation to social psychology. These are:

(i) To help the child adjust to various situations in society. This means that the child learns the various patterns of behaviour to suit social norms and ideals.

(ii) To direct the teacher to be unbiased and develop a sympathetic attitude towards his pupils.

(iii) To develop understanding about complex social relationships with the help of the principles of psychology and their application to social structure, norms and environmental situations.

(iv) To make the teachers aware of such methods which may be utilized for innovative teaching, and also for solving problems of classroom teaching.

(v) To make teachers ready for day-to-day assessment of their own teaching.

(vi) To analyse the teacher's own behaviour towards their pupils, parents and also towards bodies governing the institution, and above all, the nation.

Functions of Educational Psychology as an Academic Discipline

Educational psychology has to perform several functions as an academic subject. It has to deal with the pros and cons concerning human behaviour. It analyses information experienced through observation and field investigation. It aims to theorize knowledge and to seek principles. Its methodology is capable of carrying out investigation to discover relevant facts for testing hypotheses and deriving theories. It is a problem-solving discipline arising out of the teacher-pupil social relationship and also methodology.

Value of Psychology for Teachers

Psychology is most valuable for teachers and for their teaching process. It makes an individual know his or her capabilities and ability to perform a particular action. Everybody cannot be a teacher, a businessman, technician, or a medical practitioner. All professions require a definite skill to perform duties. Therefore, it is educational psychology which makes one aware of one's skill. It is essential to understand oneself to become a teacher. For a successful teacher, it is essential to self-assess and see whether he or she possesses the skill required for the teaching profession. A teacher must have a knowledge of psychology. It helps him to know his own aptitude and mental level. It also helps in making adjustments with colleagues and with the social environment.

Psychological knowledge helps a teacher understand the child. A child is like a raw material which can be turned into a product of social significance by an adequate knowledge of psychology. John Adams, therefore, stated that a teacher must understand the psychology of children. This is more advantageous than to be a master of the discipline of his choice. The behaviour, needs, interests, capacities, personality, etc., of children can be understood through the study of psychology. A teaching process must be based on facts of psychology such as the child's instincts, motives, emotions or his total personality.

Methods of Teaching

Teaching methods too have a psychological bearing. John Dewey is of the opinion that methods which make children learn are invariably psychological. He has suggested a tripolar relationship among methods and the teaching process. The three ingredients as suggested are: teacher, learner and curriculum. The trio forms a scientific learning process and the objective may be verified by any academician without any subjectivity. Child, teacher and the material for infusing understanding and skill form the constructive product.

The teacher during the ancient period used to be an important guide and had to play an important role. But in modern times, the learner is important rather than the teacher. The teacher is only a motivating and guiding factor in the class who leads the learner towards the goal. The learning process or methods of teaching are psychological and are based on precise informations leading to objectives. The teacher may help his pupils spell out the objectives in terms of the behaviour to be developed. He also uses tests and techniques which may exactly find out the outcomes and, finally, knows to what extent the desired objectives have been fulfilled. Thus, the entire process of the trio is psychological and scientific, and is generally termed experimental in nature.

Figure 1.1

Tripolar Relationship

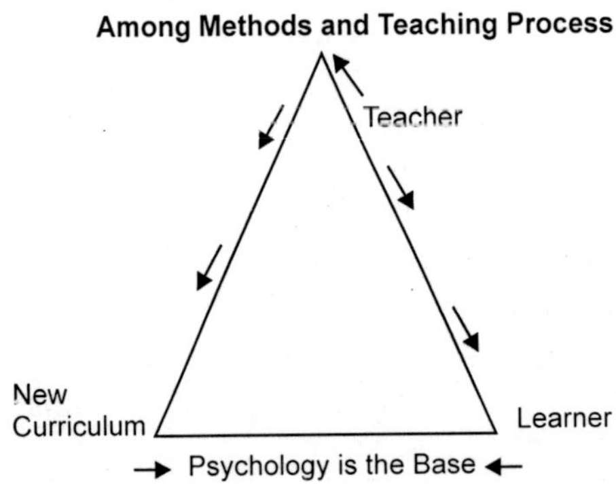

Teacher handles the situation of learner through New Curriculum, which is based on psychology of the learner.

Source: John Dewey

Among modern methods, the one which is known as 'normative' is being used widely to evaluate groups. The data is collected through various techniques like standard tests, interview, checklist, questionnaire, inventory, anecdotal records, biography and autobiography, socio-metric techniques, rating scales and direct observation. Here, the teacher seeks or evaluates the group based on individual differences.

The stages through which learners have to pass – infancy, childhood, young and adolescence – are evaluated by the generic or developmental method. In this case, the child has a long period of study and data is secured related to his unique period of growth. The data is investigated thoroughly and consequently, and throws light on the problems under consideration.

There is also a clinical method which is useful for pupils of disability cases, delinquent and the severely emotional. It studies specific learning personalities and pupils having behaviour difficulties or other complexities. Of course, the cases which need to be taught by clinical methods are only a few, but they require trained psychologists and education psychiatrists. Their data is also analysed through preventive mental hygiene.

It is clear from the discussion about the educational concepts of psychology that the teaching process can be improved provided the teacher becomes aware of the child's behaviour, and his attitude towards learning. Besides this, it is also essential that a person must assess his/her capabilities before he or she chooses to become a teacher. Many people choose this profession, thinking it to be an easy task and quite general in nature. Therefore, it is most necessary to evaluate one's taste, aptitude, qualities or capacities required before choosing the teaching profession.

Another important point which has been stated above is understanding the child. A teacher must know fully about the behaviour of the child. Without knowing the psychology of children, the teacher cannot guide them and cannot make them learn since the entire course of teaching is based on the children's instincts, interests, likes or dislikes and their emotions or reactions about novel ideas and knowledge. Methods which are ways and means of delivering knowledge and understanding must be psychologically oriented. These provide adequately the required information, and also make the path of comprehension smooth.

Self-evaluation

The progress made through the teaching process also needs proper evaluation. Both the child and the teacher remain anxious to know about the extent to which they have added to their knowledge and understanding. It is through evaluation that the teacher knows the result of motivation and also about the behavioural changes brought in the thinking and doing of children. Psychology helps to plan a proper method of evaluation. This may be oral, written or in the form of short questions or essay type, etc. Which of these suit to judge the progress of a learner, that depends on the psychology of children and also on the nature of the matter delivered to them. Evaluation techniques should fulfil the twin objectives: to know about children's progress as well as to judge the teacher's capabilities.

The Curriculum

The school curriculum which meets the needs of the learners, and also of their local and far-off social environment should be very well planned. It should be comprehensively planned to meet the requirements of different levels of pupils, and also individual differences. Effectiveness of the curriculum both for the individual and for the society is based on principles of psychology.

Problems in the Classroom

The following are some of the problems which a teacher generally comes across in the classroom. He has to play a rightful role:

(i) To lead and play right for seeking adjustment among the individual and group relations in the class.

(ii) To make all efforts for keeping the backward child abreast of the progress of the class work.

(iii) To make adjustment and bring into proper line the maladjusted child through reward or punishment.

(iv) To maintain proper discipline and academic environment in the class through motivation and by means of using creative methods.

(v) To provide opportunities to children so that they may develop in themselves the craze for self-motivation.

(vi) To find solutions to unusual problems like sex, and delinquent tendencies: crimes, suicide, misbehaving, etc. These may be met by having contact with parents, student-leaders, and in emergency, police help too may be sought.

Summing up the above, the study of experimental psychology proves to be of much use to tackle serious problems arising in unusual circumstances. The teacher should have adequate knowledge of human psychology. It requires both diagnosis and solution. It also demands to analyse the teacher's own methods and the ways and means to revise methods of teaching or reorient psychologically.

QUESTIONS

Problems for Discussion and Study

1. Define briefly:

   (a) Understanding

   (b) Learning

   (c) Applied Psychology

(d) Behaviouralism

(e) Personality

(f) Aims of Educational Psychology

(g) Principles of Teaching Process

2. What is the value of psychology for teachers? Discuss.
3. Why is psychology considered the most useful subject today?
4. 'Psychology offers new viewpoints.' Discuss it in the context of education and classroom teaching.
5. Point out briefly the classroom problems which are expected to come up during teaching.

References

Anderson, J.E., *The Psychology of Development and Personal Adjustment,* Henry Holt, NY, 1949.

Boring, E.G., *A History of Experimental Psychology,* Appleton-Century-Crofts, NY, 1950.

Freud, S., *The Problem of Anxiety,* Norton, NY, 1956.

Hall, C.S. et al., *Introduction to Theories of Personality,* Wiley, NY, 1985.

Hughes, A.G. and E.S. Hughes, *Learning and Teaching,* Longmans, London, 1955.

Lindgren, H.C., *Educational Psychology in the Classroom,* Wiley, NY, 1972.

Skinner, Charles E. (Ed.), *Educational Psychology,* Prentice-Hall, NJ, 1959.

Stephens, J.M., *The Psychology of Classroom Learning,* Holt, NY, 1965.

Symonds, P.M., *Dynamics of Human Adjustment,* Appleton, NY, 1946.

Thorndike, R.L., et al., *The Measurement of Intelligence,* Columbia University Press, NY, 1927.

2

Psychological Process of Learning

Methods and Scope

Teaching and Learning

Modern education is based on psychology, and the subject is totally influenced by the psychological foundation. In the previous chapter, we have sufficiently described that education is child-centred. There cannot be any teaching without basing it on the principles of child psychology. Children are like raw material in the hands of a teacher. The raw material is processed through various techniques to finally giving it the shape of a useful product. The child who enters the class with an uneven behaviour is unclear about the circumstances he or she has to face in the class. The teacher too, at the first instance, does not know about the mental make-up of the child whom he wants to change into a useful product. Here comes the role of applied psychology, which makes the child adapt to the classroom situation, and the teacher attentive towards the mental aptitude of the child. Thus, the main function of the teacher and his working in the class have their basis in children's capacities, and also the teacher's own understanding of the immature mental make-up of the children. The teacher, therefore, has to gauge the abilities of children to make them adjustable with the working of the teaching process.

Complexity of Learning Process

The process of learning involves the child, teacher and comprehension or reaction taking place in the mind of a child, whom the teacher wants to make adjustable cognitively. In other words, the learning process produces the desired reaction at a particular moment in the mind of the child. He tries to adapt to the new situation generated by the teacher. But the problem arises when certain facts are learnt by the children themselves. The child learns in the same process many things which are not taught by the teacher in the class. There may be much churning within the child during the course of learning. It is necessary, therefore, to discover what is going in the child's mind. This may give rise to some new principles and these may be useful for the teacher for further analysis to remove the difficulties and finally helping him in solving the problems. The resultant psycho-based difficulties have to be discovered. And, it is the function of the educational psychologist or teacher to be aware constantly about the complexities growing in the minds of children.

Educational psychology today has not a fixed role limited only to the teacher, but it is a continuous process going on between the teacher and the taught to remove the obstacles in solving the problems. It is a two-way process to provide experiences both to the teacher and the taught.

Psycho-based Education

Areas of Teaching

Educational psychology completes the classroom working through three components forming their own domain, but interrelated intrinsically. These are enunciated by Lindgren as learner, learning process and learning situation. In terms of education, these form the child, teacher and cognition.

The learner has the central place and the teacher processes through a scientific system to familiarize him about the phenomena characterized by cognitive skills. In the classroom, the teacher interacts with learners or their group individually and also collectively. The learners too interact with the teacher, and both carry forward the process to achieve certain goals.

Figure 2.1

Lindgren's Classroom Working

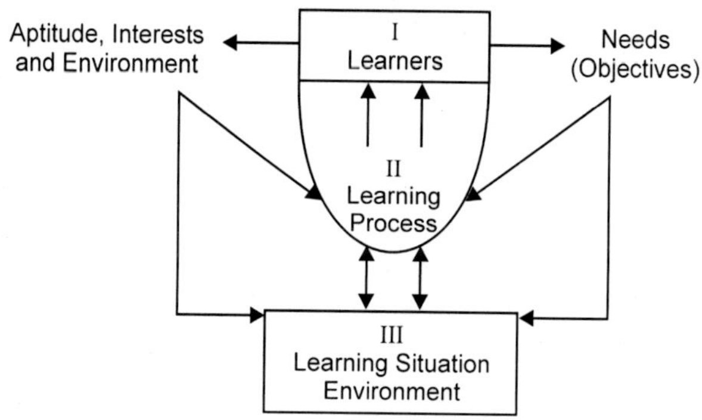

I There can be no teaching without *learners*.

II *Learning Process:* New ways of thinking and behaving.

III *Learning Situation* is the environment in which the learning process takes place.

The learner being a social unit, the process in the classroom passes through the individual-cum-social problems. The teacher remains careful about the potentialities of the children whom he aims to change, in order to be useful individually as well as socially. There may arise many hindrances in the smooth working of the classroom due to the physical and emotional climate of children, teachers and the school. The educational psychologist comes to the rescue to meet the situation with a sympathetic attitude and also through the cooperation of children and managing personalities. The educational psychologist tries to adapt to various situations to meet the needs of the children, the teacher and the process of learning through the aims and objectives of education. In other words, the psychologist tries to overhaul the outlook of the student and the educator by emphasizing on achieving the objectives.

Aims and Objectives

The aims and objectives of psycho-based education have basically two foundations: wholesome personality development and continuous stage-by-stage growth of children. An important point of view is to aim to help the teacher in the process of teaching so that he or she may understand the human nature. Teaching does not aim simply to add to knowledge, but to bring about changes in the behaviour of children so that they may prove to be useful for the society. Children must develop ideas and adjust themselves according to the ideal norms for social good. They must be made to think positively. They need proper guidance so that they may prove to be a useful unit and may act responsively as per the needs and values of the social environment.

The task of the psycho-based teaching process is to equip the teacher and reinforce him by providing facts which may help children develop their personality wholesomely. The aims, thus, are to develop:

(i) Proper attitude in the teacher for dealing with educational problems. He can learn adequate means to face situations in the classroom, and may use the experiences gained to train children's behaviour to adapt to the social order.

(ii) To help the teacher in developing a sympathetic attitude. The teacher must develop a viewpoint to study the child's behaviour objectively. This is only possible when he remains unbiased and unattached in his treatment of children.

(iii) To train the teacher so that he may plan and organize the teaching material according to children's psychology.

(iv) To have the capacities and capabilities of participating and also organizing adequate activities so that these may develop a sense of social good. The teacher's role in co-curricular activities affects positively the classroom working.

Psycho-based methods help the teacher in analysing his own behaviour towards children and these also provide clues to analyse others' behaviour too. The teacher must develop proper guidance techniques. These techniques differ in dealing with the individual traits of children.

Summing up, the general aim of psycho-based education is to develop a wholesome personality in the child. It is a balanced personality which generates in the child the capacity for self-motivation to work for his own development and also for that of the society with fullest zeal.

The particular aims of educational psychology are adjustment in social behaviour, unbiased sympathetic attitude towards the child, understanding of the nature and importance of social relationships, solving problems arising in the classroom, to develop insights for assessing own teaching, and also his own behaviour and that of others.

Figure 2.2

Psychological Teaching

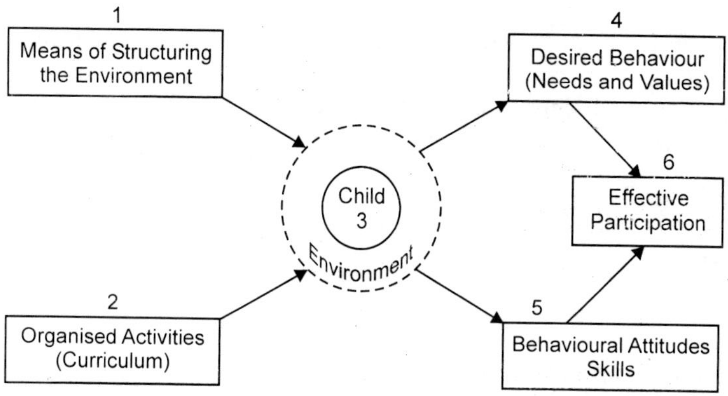

Process of Psychological Education and Its Functions

Bases of Psychological Teaching

The chief characteristic or foundation of psychological teaching is the child, who is the centre of the teaching process. Everything in the classroom is not so important as the child, whom the teacher wants to mould. The process of teaching, the curriculum, methods, etc., all are planned according to the psychological bent of the child's mind.

The process of teaching has to orient the nature of the student, the teacher and the subject to be taught. The educator has to understand both the student and the subject. Thus, the teacher must study the child and should orient his methods of teaching for the likes-dislikes of the child. The teacher must utilize every opportunity psychologically to make the child feel at home and to familiarize him with various environments.

Children have many individual traits. Some are slow and some are fast. Children have different tastes and there are differences in their attitudes, qualities or abilities that form their personalities. Hence, various personality traits are present among children which the teacher has to deal with. Heredity and influence of environment too play an important role in the physical and mental development of children, nature and rate of learning, interests, aptitude, etc. Psychological bases, as applied to the different traits, train the student to help him in devising his ways and means of achieving the right attitude.

The problem of individual characteristics among children is met through the introduction of various plans such as Dalton plan, project method, Vinetka method, contact plan, activity programme, etc. These plans teach individuals by providing different tasks in the projects. In this process, different kinds of children are taught.

Now, the process of education has totally changed. The impact of psychology has now made education child-centred. It is now established that discipline in the class cannot be maintained by the rule of rod, or by thrashing or suppressing the child. Something better can be thought to introduce self-discipline among children through monitoring. By all efforts and means, the process of teaching and learning has to be made entertaining and interesting. This should be taken as granted that education is something which cannot be forced from outside, rather it is a system which needs to be developed keeping in mind the child's aptitude. It needs to seek adjustment with the changed social environment.

Primary Education

A child should not be treated like an adult, but through child psychology. Every child possesses different perception, attention span, imagination and concepts. Therefore, the education of a child needs the complete understanding about his or her behaviour and personality. Infancy is the most critical stage and the impressions once made last forever. Education during infancy period is most important. Primary education must be in the hands of the most capable teachers, having psychological training. It is not enough to make the education of primary stage universal and compulsory. The educators of primary sections should be given all sorts of facilities, financial as well as material. Individual attention to every student is the need of the hour. It is only possible by restricting the number of pupils in one class so that each student gets personal attention. Each child has its own personality and he or she needs psychological guidance for dealing with the hurdles and solving the problems. Contemporary education needs a revolutionary change in the light of child psychology and methods of learning.

Education with Psychological Bearing

When education is treated practically in the classroom, it becomes applied science. It deals with human behaviour and experience with particular reference to students. The behavioural aspect is the subject of psychology and, therefore, classroom teaching is associated with applied psychology. The process applies facts of teaching to actual life conditions of students in the classroom. Applied psychology in relation to facts of education is mainly concerned with problems of pupils and their solutions. The teacher during the classroom teaching attempts to change students' attitude and behaviour in view of the objectives. This is actually an attempt to develop a balanced personality of the child. Thc tcacher makes use of facts collected out of human behaviour and experiences of the system of teaching in the classroom.

Education with psychological learning as applied to the child's behaviour brings to fore many problems faced by the teacher, and some have been pointed out in the following paragraphs:

(i) Development of a balanced personality in the child is the crucial aspect that the teacher attempts to seek. A balanced personality is blended by cognitive values as well as social, moral and emotional aspects. Certain traits within the child are his weakest links and some equally important and useful qualities are hidden unused. Such children behave awkwardly. There are some who are known as spoilt ones, and behave excessively indecently and awfully. Some avoid social norms and remain in the dreamy world of their own. Such personalities are distorted and unbalanced. They may be treated with applied psychological notion to bring them finally in the normal course of having a balanced behaviour tinge.

(ii) Another important problem the teacher generally faces in the classroom is about the slow learner or backward child. It is necessary to bring such students into the general process of learning to keep pace with the rest of the classmates. This happens when the teaching process is without motivation. It is essential that to keep progress of all sorts of pupils, some motivation is necessary to punctuate the teaching-pupil interaction. Reinforcement, motivation, appreciation and praise are psychological elements which keep the process of teaching accelerated and the classroom graph line shows an upward or rising trend of progress everyday. These elements create a healthy competition among the children.

(iii) It depends upon the teacher to select adequate material and present it by means of audio-visual aids so that pupils become involved completely and grasp the situation, howsoever complex it may be. The teacher must be careful about the solutions to intricate problems. And this is only possible if the teacher takes into consideration the familiar environment with which the pupils are related. Dramatic and mock-based activities are forms of motivation which engage all sorts of pupils. They comprehend and understand the implications of the problem in hand.

The psycho-based teaching process invigorates cognitive learning and makes children interested in the situations favourable to them. The teacher considers the nature of learners, their level of maturity, their individual characteristics, relation between the teaching material and methods of exposition and also the capacities of learners to adapt to the new social and cultural circumstances. Psychology has revolutionized education in the sense that it revolves around the learning process to deal with individual differences and nature of the learner. It also brings forth the possibilities of the child's all-round development and his capabilities for seeking social adjustment.

Methods of Educational Psychology

Educational psychology is based primarily on two methods: observation and exposition.

Observation Method

Observation may be introspective and also objective. Introspection means that an individual analyses his own mental process. In other words, it is self-observation. Introspection includes three steps, viz., (i) individual thinks about his own mental process, (ii) he scrutinizes his own actions, and (iii) he thinks of the ways and means for mental activities. This method is unsound scientifically because the same phenomenon may be interpreted differently by different persons. It is highly subjective because the mental condition is constantly changing.

Objective Observation

In an objective observation, the activities and actions of another person are studied. This is also subjective because the observer may describe his own views in describing the behaviour of another person.

Experimental Method

In this method, the process of learning is studied under controlled conditions. A definite variable is selected for investigation. The laboratory is kept free. The definite variable is a particular mental activity which is artificially created by manipulating the situation. This method too has its drawbacks because the mental process cannot be fully controlled. The behaviour of the individual is uncertain, and it is not like an 'object'. Experimental psychology studies the behaviour of certain objects as physical science. But, an individual's behaviour cannot be an object. We cannot be rigid in case of understanding the behaviour of children. Experimental psychology cannot be of much use to educational problems. It fails to assess feelings and emotions of children objectively.

Besides observation, there are certain other methods which are descriptive, and are known as *methods of exposition*. Some of these are given here:

Development or Genetic Method

This method studies the child's mental process at different stages of development, i.e., at birth, at childhood, at adolescence, etc. It is a method of studying human behaviour in its natural setting. It brings forth useful information about the mental make-up of the individual at different stages of development. Therefore, it is generally used in case of persons showing undesirable behaviour. It can resolve the present complexes of the individual by knowing his past emotional disturbances. The genetic method is generally used by child psychologists because the development of the child is generally based on heredity and environmental influences.

The Case History Method

This method gives us clues about the peculiarities of a particular individual. A complete history of the individual is gathered and it brings to light the qualities, drawbacks and even his abnormalities. It is very useful to study criminal, insane or neurotic individuals. Police stations generally keep a record of criminals which is used during emergency, disturbances and cases of murder or thefts, etc.

The clinical psychologists and also homeopaths diagnose the problem of the patient by the case history. The history of the client includes all sorts of information such as nomenclature of self, parents, residence, age, sex, nationality, caste, religion, membership of associations, parties, occupation, religious or non-religious attitude, education, marital relations and information about his movements, outings, travels, sources of income, profession, etc.

The Comparative Method

Under this method, various types of behaviour of an individual are compared with those of another person. The study of different animals is also compared, and a comparison is also made between men and animals to delineate human behaviour and character. Man and animal are governed by common biological laws. It is because of this that the branch of animal psychology has also been developed.

The Sociometric Method

It is used generally in social research. But it is very helpful in understanding school conditions where social and non-social pupils take part in group activities. It is the technique which covers all members of the group. In a group, some members accept the activity while some reject it. The likes and dislikes can be the measure of locating the most favoured ones, and also the least accepted activities. The teacher can also locate socially-isolated cases among groups of pupils. He can arrange and plan for such members a better group with favourable alliances.

Freud's Psycho-analytic Method

According to Freud, 7/8th part of the mind is unconscious and the remaining 1/8th is conscious. The unconscious part is developed through unpleasant experiences and it controls the behaviour of the individual. He becomes neurotic. It causes unsound development, and through analysis of his dreams and free conversations, the inner feelings and inferences are drawn. If the inner feelings are analysed correctly, his abnormality may disappear.

Pathological or Clinical Method

It is the method which can help in finding out the causes of the mental disease. All types of abnormality can be studied by the clinical method and, therefore, it is very commonly used by pathologists.

Use of Methods for Psychological Education

These methods are a subject of psychology, and thus these may prove useful in deciding the nature of human behaviour. These can also be of much use to improve the teaching process and behaviour of children. Delinquent children when put to clinical tests may reveal the circumstances of their mischiefs and undesirable activities. Psychological education can suggest devices for dealing with them. The teacher may use these to bring abnormal children on the right track. They need sympathy and some constructive activities to develop a normal behaviour about the results of their ill-habits.

Scope of Educational Psychology

Educational psychology has its basis in the student, the educator and the process of teaching. It is entirely a science dealing with the behaviour of human beings. Therefore, educational psychology has a very wide field to deal with. In the process of psychological teaching, it has to get help from many other subjects which are related to children's activities and their entire life. The process of teaching prepares children for their proper adjustment with the physical and social environments, and also orients them to prove to be a useful unit of society and also for the nation.

The learning process is related with the science of biology, physiology and sociology. The successful learning process is possible only when the child's physical, motor, social, emotional and mental growth is taken into consideration. The physiological and biological domains are very much concerned with the sex, height and weight, age, etc., though the rate of growth of children in these aspects is different.

Educational psychology is also related with the maturity of the brain and that of the whole nervous system. It takes into consideration the child's mental growth. Biology and physiology thus fall under the scope of psychological basis of education since these provide clues for growth and development.

To conclude, the scope of psychological education is very wide. The scope primarily includes the child, the teacher and society. The teacher prepares the child to make him a useful unit of society. He moulds the child's behaviour and makes his personality balanced. The techniques employed for the child's development to make him adjust in the physical and social environments and also to make him vocationally fit are called learning methods. These methods are based on the child's innate behaviour. Thus, the entire process covers a wide scope and includes family, neighbourhood, social and national panorama.

QUESTIONS

Short Answer Type Questions

1. Define 'educational psychology'.
2. What is the use of educational psychology?
3. Define province of educational psychology.
4. Define teacher and taught relationship.
5. Point out major areas of psycho-based teaching.
6. Briefly discuss the complexities of the learning process.

Average Answer Type Questions

1. What are psycho-based aims of teaching children?
2. Discuss major characteristics of a wholesome personality.
3. Explain the bases of psycho-based teaching.
4. What do you mean by human behaviour as developed in the classroom by the teacher?
5. Discuss merits and demerits of observation method.

Essay Type Questions

1. Methods of Educational Psychology.
2. Scope of Educational Psychology.
3. Psycho-based Teaching Learning Process.

References

Eson, M.E., *Psychological Foundations of Education*, Holt, NY, 1964.
Fraser, D.K., *The Psychology of Education*, Methuen, London, 1944.
Lindgren, H.C., *Educational Psychology in the Classroom*, Wiley, NY, 1972.
Ruch, F.L., *Psychology and Life*, Scott, Foreman & Co., Chicago, 1963.
Stephens, J.M., *The Psychology of Classroom Learning*, Holt, NY, 1965.
Woodworth, R.S., *Psychology*, Holt, NY, 1947.

3

Inherent Powers of a Child

Powers of the Mind

R.S. McDougall believes that the behaviour of a human being is not mechanical. His activities are the result of some motives. Behaviourists think that human acts are guided by reflex action or these are machine-like. But this is not correct, and, there is a lot of difference in the acts of organisms and material objects. Actions of individuals or their behaviour and also of a child cannot be called lifeless, and thus, these are not mechanical. Behaviour of individuals is guided by their mind and it must be different from those material objects which are not controlled by the power of mind. Mind possesses certain powers. These are psychologically known as innate or inherent basic powers. These are beneficial for mental experiences of an individual. Educational psychologists believe that the child's mind possesses three kinds of powers: (a) Mneme, (b) Horme, and (c) Cohesion.

Mneme

This power is known as the collection of impressions received by the child's mind. It is said that a child begins to have impressions even before the birth during pregnancy. It is the power through which the child starts to learn and the child's mind retains the impressions. The child identifies the mother's lap as soon as he or she takes birth and feels very comfortable. The power of mneme, as called by Percy Nunn, leaves permanent impressions on the mind; and without it, learning is not possible. This innate power is different from memory. Memory does not leave permanent impressions. It may disappear later on, but mneme gradually refines the impressions which are retained in the mind as past behaviour. It is, therefore, also called 'engram'. Its field is wide enough for retaining lots of experiences in our mind. But memory's field is restricted. This power is responsible for developing good impressions in our mind. The teacher during the course of the teaching process tries to promote good impressions and leaves no opportunity when these are expressed, as time and place allow. A good or intelligent teacher can make the child cultured and positive or an ideal citizen with the help of the power of mneme.

Horme

Man always acts with a purpose. It is the power of mind that invokes the child to act with a purpose. Materials or objects also do or perform acts but their action is purposeless and mechanical. An individual's mind has one or the other purpose. Man possesses a motive to act and it is present in his conscious or unconscious mind. It makes him act with purpose. McDougall believed that there cannot be any action which has no purpose behind the mind of an individual. Even the smallest organism has some purpose behind the action. Therefore, educational psychologists believe that actions of human beings are governed by the power of horme.

The educational value of the power of horme is significant. An intelligent teacher utilizes instinctive behaviour and makes the same purposive in which the child shows interest. McDougall has discussed 14 instincts which generate purposive action in individuals. The teacher may make his teaching process purposeful by correlating some instincts. This motivates the child and he or she shows a lot of enthusiasm in learning the purposeful matter of the course.

Cohesion

The power of cohesion is hereditary. The power of cohesion develops order, coherence and system in a child's mind. He retains impressions and these are helpful in solving problems provided it is systematized thinking. It is the power of cohesion which helps the child to systematize and classify various impressions. The impressions and experiences when they come in contact with the past impression, these form a complex called 'engram'. This complex is the base of mental activities. It develops a system and thereby makes a child work systematically and culturally. It is actually the power of cohesion which gradually brings refinement in men's actions. A teacher also tries to make use of the power of cohesion. He tries to make each new thing that he teaches coherent with past experiences. The previous knowledge of the child is utilized to make him conversant with the new facts. Cohesion facilitates recalling. It is known as the association of ideas, and an experienced teacher makes use of this power of the mind.

Natural Tendencies: Instincts

Each individual is born with certain powers which motivate him for purposive actions. Individual behaviour and actions are a consequence of inborn powers. He or she behaves differently in different situations. In the language of psychology, instincts are motivating powers which invigorate an individual to behave in natural situations. Instinctive behaviour can only be released by a specific type of stimulus. According to McDougall, "instincts are inherited or innate psychophysical disposition which determines its possessor to perceive and to pay attention to objects of a certain class, to experience an emotional excitement of a particular quality upon perceiving such an object and to act in regard to it in a particular manner or at least to experience an impulse to such an action".

It is clear from the above definition that instincts are innate tendencies. It is a generated behaviour which concentrates a person's attention on some particular objects. The instinctive attention passes through three stages: (a) cognitive aspect, i.e., to attend to and to be interested in certain types of objects or situations; (b) affective aspect, or to feel certain emotion towards these objects; and (c) conative aspect or to act towards them in a particular way.

But it must be understood that every instinct cannot be activated at any time or by any type of stimulus. This means that a particular instinctive behaviour is a result of a specific type of stimulus.

Instincts are not emotions. McDougall defines emotion as the mode of experience that accompanies the working of an instinctive impulse. In the following table, McDougall ascribes the related emotions to all of the 14 instincts:

Table 3.1

Instincts and Related Emotions

Instinct	*Accompanying Emotion*
Escape	Fear
Repulsion	Disgust
Curiosity	Wonder
Pugnacity	Anger
Self-Assertion	Positive self-feeling
Self-Abasement	Subjection
Parental	Tender emotion
Gregariousness	Loneliness
Acquisitiveness	Feeling of ownership
Constructiveness	Feeling of creativeness
Food seeking	Appetite
Sex	Lust
Appeal	Distress
Laughter	Amusement

Instinct and Reflex Action

Instinct and reflex action are not one and the same. Instinct is a complex in which a person reacts as a whole to the situation. An instinctive person is fully excited when he attacks. But reflex action is localized in a part of the body, like when withdrawing the hand on being pricked by a pin. The hand immediately moves to remove the flies from the nose or from any part of the face. The reflex action takes place unconsciously. But instincts are persistence and a steady activity. Instinctive behaviour works towards certain aims, while reflex activity is unconsciously done. The instinctive activities include the mental elements, e.g., interest, attention, maturity and learning by experience. The difference between instinct and reflex action can be tabulated as below:

Table 3.2

Behavioural Contrast between Instinctive Activity and Reflex Action

Instinctive Activity	*Reflex Action*
Complex	Simple
Of long duration	Momentary
Many stimuli	One stimulus
Knowledge of aims	Unconsciously done
Changeable	Unchangeable
Mental element	Absence of mental element

Instincts and Education

Instinct is a constant tendency towards a particular class of objects. It can also be modified for its favourable expression. Sex instinct of a male towards the female can be sublimated when its repercussions are expressed and its disagreeable experiences are brought forward. Some boys and girls because of disagreeable situations destroy their future life. The teacher can make use of such instances to sublimate the natural instinct of sex, and, it may develop fear or hatred rather than lust. The instinct may become inactive because of moral and social fears.

In the classroom, an experienced and intelligent teacher can sublimate 'escape' which is associated with the emotion of fear by arousing repulsion for indecent and unknown scenes, acts or traditions. The pugnacity or combat among classmates is usual, and the teacher can use his decision to bring the involved groups at rest and adjust with the situation. For this type of combat, conflicts and undesirable competitions, the best outlet to sublimate pugnacity are games. Games create a healthy discipline, including mental equilibrium.

The teacher should not interfere unnecessarily with the routine of a pupil's classwork. If the child feels interference and is stopped from doing things on his own, he may get annoyed and it may mount anger in him. The teacher must take into consideration the nature of the child before assigning him a task. It should not be beyond his ability. Parents and teachers both should behave with their wards fairly. If the teacher shows favouritism to one and unconcernedness to the other, this may cause irritation among the sufferers.

The teacher should introduce new situations gradually and not abruptly. The suddenness of new learning techniques may develop fear. An intelligent teacher may ask his pupils to introspect after a bad situation is over. A student may probably realize that his action was inappropriate. The anger or adverse situations may be avoided or improved by self-assessment.

It is the law of hedonism that human beings select pleasant objects and activities by nature. The teacher may make use of it and award the instinctive motivated behaviour. At the same time, he should also be careful to punish for unpleasant behaviour in the class. But psychologists do not agree with the negative approach of punishment. It may cease the child's development, they argue.

The process of education may transform instincts in human behaviour by repression, inhibition, contradiction, reduction and through sublimation. Undesirable instincts are generally suppressed. Their repression gradually makes them disappear out of the conscious mind. Their disappearance may also cause deprivation of the creative powers and energy. For example, the normal and healthy sex instinct generally creates in man tremendous energy. And, if these instincts are denied satisfaction, an individual will be deprived of creative powers. Extreme repression of instincts prevents normal development of individual personality and character.

The law of inhibition can also transform instincts. It contends that if instinct does not get a chance to find expression, gradually it ceases to exist. But educational psychologists believe that inhibition does not kill instincts. These are changed when they leave their domain of the conscious mind, and continue to exist in the unconscious world. The teacher has immense opportunities to utilize the unconscious part of children's mind.

Contradiction is an easy way and good method of transforming instincts for good. For example, the sex instinct can be best utilized by providing due respect and honour to women by men. In modern times, people are advised to recognize the achievement of the opposite sex, and develop brotherly feelings and affectionate relations. The instinct of combat may also be controlled by propagating universal brotherhood in this tension-ridden world.

Redirecting instincts is the best method of transforming for the good and welfare of human beings. The instinct in this mode of transformation is completely changed. Combative instinct is now successfully employed constructively by providing due rights – political, financial and educational, etc., to backward classes, and by guarding the weak and protecting the oppressed. The teachers of civics, sociology, and economics may plan their teaching lessons by utilizing the method of redirection of instincts. They may create an environment of brotherhood, friendliness, international peace and healthy economic and balanced trade relations by harnessing fear, disgust, anger, subjection, feeling of ownership, creativeness and amusement.

Changing the form of instinct through sublimation, according to McDougall, "is a process by which the energies of our instinctive nature are utilized on higher planes of acting than the instinctive". Sublimation helps to divert the instinct from its normal expression to a superior moral direction for better social welfare.

To sum up the significance of instincts, the success of a child's education and the development of an individual has the basis in utilization of proper opportunities when instincts are transformed and sublimated. The process of transformation of instincts may be gradual but should be constant. The transformed instincts and their emotions can clear the obstacles and an individual can make easy adjustment with his social environment.

Imitation

Almost all children imitate their elders' actions and it is also one of the natural tendencies found in individuals. Describing its characteristic, McDougall has pointed out that "it is copying by an individual of the actions, the bodily movements of another individual". It is seen that sons imitate their father's talk and walk, their writing and also expression of ideas, thoughts, etc. Psychologists have characterized imitation as the conscious emulation of the behaviour and conduct of others.

Types of Imitation

McDougall has classified imitation into five types:

1. *Sympathetic Imitation:* If an individual is sympathetic towards any child, it is commonly seen that the child starts emulating his actions. This type of imitation is generally physical or psychological.
2. *Ideo-motor Imitation:* When any idea crops up in your mind, you begin to work on the idea. There is little difference between the time of occurrence of the idea and the activity. You act immediately as soon as the idea occurs in your mind. It is a sort of unconscious behaviour, and there is almost no gap of time between the idea and the imitated action accordingly.
3. *Deliberate Imitation:* It is wilful imitation and is based on one's interests and objectives. If an individual has an interest in cricket, he exerts in his efforts to handle the bat and ball in his room without any supervision. He prepares initially and imitates techniques of playing cricket by indulging in practice alone day and night. Actually, he is self-motivated by his interest to become a player of the game. Someone wants to be an orator. He exerts to learn to deliver the speech and practices by standing before the looking-glass in his own room. It is his will and interest that motivate him to act, and for the success he initially practices, thus imitating the technique of the desired activity.
4. *Intermediary Imitation:* This type of imitation is characterized by ideo-motor or interest of children for an aimless and prior thought. Children play the role of 'police thief' or 'rail engine and guard' or the 'king and his subject'. There may be any scene or situation which appeals to children. They imitate the situation through the power of their imagination.
5. *Meaningless Imitation:* Infants imitate without any meaning in the act. It is natural imitation, and later on this may become an important source of the child's social behaviour patterns. It is very much the same as described under the deliberate type. The difference is that an infant's imitation has no idea or interest. It is just like a natural activity performed meaninglessly.

Imitation and Education

Educationally, the concept of imitation is significant. It is because of the fact of imitating their peers that the children's behaviour is enriched and they become experienced. Primarily, children's education is given through imitation. Children learn speaking and pronouncing words correctly by imitating their teacher's pronouncing style. Teachers-to-be during the course of their training are constantly told by their supervisors to pronounce words correctly while demonstrating the lessons of language. The writing by the teacher in the classroom on the blackboard must be uniform, equally-spaced, well-worded, clear, meaningful and correct. It is generally imitated by the children. The teacher's dress, habits of speech and the materials handled in the class should have a scientific base so that the pupils too may learn of an adequate system in the classroom. The teacher's behaviour influences very much his or her pupils. Therefore, the teacher must be careful and should try to present an ideal before the students.

Competition among pupils is very natural. Each of the students tries to get ahead. This is good but envy should not come in the way of competition. The teacher must guard against this. Let pupils emulate, but without developing envious relations and combat-bearing situations.

Imitation is the medium of social norms, ideals, customs and traditions. Pupils carry these from one generation to the next. An able teacher can succeed in moulding the behaviour of the students on the basis of positive cultural traditions.

Sympathy

Sympathy means sharing the pains and pleasures with another individual. The act of sympathy is visible in our day-to-day experience. Our behaviour towards others can be sympathetic or non-sympathetic or unconcerned. It is essential to be emotional, if you want to exhibit sympathy. It is a natural behaviour and according to McDougall, it is not an emotion but an instinct.

Sympathy and gregariousness are innate tendencies and make social life possible. It is natural that one feels pained when he or she finds someone in distress. Sympathy possesses an uneven power of expression. It influences differently in different situations and also by different types of people. Someone sees a beggar or a physically-challenged person and feels sympathetic and tries to help him, while others pass by unconcernedly, gossiping with their friends. Thus, the velocity of sympathetic feeling is uneven and it is variedly found in individuals.

To express sympathy, one does not need thinking. It is mostly situation-bound. When someone sees another person weeping, laughing or in an angry mood, he expresses pain or pleasure. McDougall has expressed in his treatise 'Social Psychology' that one can observe the existence of sympathy arising out of emotion and feeling. This feeling is gradually developed. In infants, its form is different and its expression generally is found in crying and yelling. But at later stages, children communicate this in the form of fear, curiosity and anger. Therefore, McDougall opines that children possess a natural tendency towards sympathy for others.

Sympathy is both acquired and innate. It can be motivated by instinct. And, at the same time, it is a natural reaction to the situation. In fact, man has acquired sympathetic behaviour in society and, it is not simply instinctive. A child learns to sympathize by imitating the behaviour of his parents or elders. Thus, it can be said that there is much in sympathy that is acquired and much that is innate.

Sympathy and Education

In education, sympathy has a significant role to play. The child learns easily if he is taught sympathetically. Sympathy is also the key to solve problems in the class. The child should be taught to behave sympathetically with classmates and equals. Sympathy helps in the study of history, literature, and artistic disciplines like dancing, music, paintings, etc.

Sympathy should be extended only to those who deserve it. The teacher must develop it for the distressed, poor and handicapped and the children should be made to learn to help them sympathetically. Psychologists believe that sympathy is a sort of motivation and during the class teaching, adequate reinforcement must be provided for children for their intelligent response. It may develop a positive character in children. The teacher should show adequate sympathy for the class monitor, leader and also for slow learners at the right moment or whenever the opportunity arises.

Suggestion

Suggestion is a process of mind carrying ideas of one individual to influence and mould others' inappropriate ideas. It is a process to communicate a proposition for acceptance without any logic. It is a natural act and people accept suggestions of peers without any hitch. This tendency is commonly found in all individuals. Children at once accept the suggestion of elders and particularly of their teachers. They are generally seen influenced by elders, peers and intelligent people. They accept their suggestions without thinking of the pros and cons. Younger children may be misled easily because they accept elders' suggestions without any hitch.

Suggestions are often accepted quickly in the special bodily circumstances. For example, weak and diseased people accept suggestions of sturdy and healthy personalities. In the classroom, pupils accept suggestions of their teachers because the latter are considered mentally mature. Similarly, the students who are weak in the class, accept suggestions of intelligent classmates. People who have gained respect, leaders and learned professors influence the masses with their suggestions and ideas easily. Leaders like Mahatma Gandhi and Jawaharlal Nehru, social workers and philosopher-saints like Swami Vivekanand, Swami Dayanand, Ramkrishna Paramhans influenced masses with their suggestive ideology because of the respect and faith they commanded.

The teacher should welcome the suggestions of the pupils and give them full attention. A good teacher is really one who while keeping all the time the leadership in his hands, can shift it at will to develop a spirit of comradeship among his pupils without losing his prestige.

The degree of suggestions accepted differs from person to person. Its percentage degree can be calculated as:

$$Suggestibility = \frac{No.\ of\ accepted\ suggestions}{No.\ of\ suggestions\ given} \times 100$$

Similarly, coefficient of suggestibility can also be easily found by dividing the number of accepted suggestions by the total number of suggestions given:

$$\textit{Coefficient of Suggestibility} = \frac{\textit{No. of accepted suggestions}}{\textit{No. of suggestions given}}$$

Education and Forms of Suggestions

There are many types of suggestions which are commonly advanced. But educationally, a teacher comes across in the class different types of suggestions, such as:

1. *Ideo-motor suggestions:* In the classroom, pupils act and respond as soon as an idea crops up in their mind. Therefore, during the teaching process, when a teacher throws an idea, the pupils act immediately without giving time for its discussion or for logical thinking. The suggestion is unconsciously accepted. There is no discrimination between the idea thrown and action. But this is not of much use in the classroom. Ideas must be discussed before they are converted into action. Interaction between teacher and pupils is necessary.
2. *Prestige suggestions:* These are received from the elders and from prestigious people. In the classroom, the teacher being the academic leader holds the prestigious position. He is a specialist and well-versed. His views are easily accepted. But many teachers forfeit their right by being diffident or hesitant or by showing embarrassment. This is an awkward situation and his or her suggestions are not fully welcomed. The result is chaos in the class.
3. *Auto-suggestions:* A powerful thinker develops auto-suggestion and accepts the character that he or she develops and the thoughts that he entertains. The power of thinking makes you confident and you develop faith. Thus, doctor also advises the patient to have faith in his cure. This belief helps to influence the health favourably. Great men possess high ideals and in the time of adversity, they reassure themselves that they would be successful in their motive. Auto-suggestions have an important role to play and the teacher makes all efforts to develop self-sufficiency in children and they are motivated to develop confidence.

4. *Mass suggestions* mean receiving suggestions of the same nature from a number of persons. Many people suggest the same clues to a child to solve a problem. He becomes almost insane and falls prey to mass suggestion. When several teachers appear before a class and address the students about permanent values of truth, beauty and good, the pupils become assured about the suggestions and receive them favourably.
5. *Contra-suggestions* are not effective in the sense that often children act against the suggestion put again and again by their teacher. There are people who seek pleasure in contradicting suggestions of their co-workers. When you warn the pupils not to open the box lying in a corner of their classroom, they inevitably try to open it. In other words, if you forbid something, there arouses a curiosity to act contrary to the command. It is common among children.
6. *Direct suggestions* are of a direct nature and pupils are aware of it. A teacher asks pupils to complete their pending work or when he asks students to revise the lesson taught today, the suggestion is clear and reveals the intention.
7. *Indirect suggestions* are not quite apparent and the intention is not clear for accepting these. Such suggestions make a greater impression upon the pupils.
8. *Positive suggestions* are made to obey some order; for example, the teacher asks students to come on time in the class or to make no noise in the class.
9. *Negative suggestions* are made for rejecting some idea or not to follow the path leading to a course of particular action.

Educational Significance of Suggestions

A teacher should make all efforts through suggestions in the class to invoke pupils to achieve self-knowledge. New knowledge may be given to students by providing adequate suggestions. The teacher should explore devices of providing suggestions so that complex problems and facts may be explained comprehensibly. As far as possible, teachers should try to correlate situations with the day-to-day life and make suggestions accordingly. Suggestions should be either in the form of questions or questions framed with prepared charts and pictures. Putting questions based on charts provides opportunities for thinking and develops in pupils the skill of interpretation. It develops the power of self-work and activity.

Suggestions are provided with great care in the class and due precautions should be taken. There should not be unnecessary and unlimited suggestions. This creates difficulties in developing the independent power of thinking among pupils. Suggestions are unique devices and these must not be unnecessarily provided. The misuse of suggestions hinders the power of self-thinking.

Suggestive questions and questions having answers either in 'yes' or 'no' should be avoided. The suggestions which bear answers are as far as possible to be avoided.

Play Tendency

Play is an innate tendency. In educational psychology, play is significant. It is a harbinger of spontaneity, freedom and joy. It is found equally in children, youngsters and adults. It fosters development of mental powers and physique. According to McDougall, play is a natural tendency like suggestion or imitation.

Modern education is mainly based on play. Young one of birds and animals too play. Children and adults, all are interested in some kind of play. Throw a ball before a pup, and see how it runs after the ball and tries to catch it. You may also find a lone child playing, and he plays with others too.

Playing for a child is as necessary as food or water and he cannot live without it. It is a natural activity and one of the drives of human life. A child learns through play various social qualities like rights and duties, justice, truth and joy, competition and friendliness, self-protection and health.

Play is different from work. Work is done with a definite aim. Play is only to play and players get joy. But when we play for money, and players are hired for this purpose, it becomes work.

Theories of Play

The following theories of play show that play too has some purpose.

1. *Surplus Energy Theory:* Friedreich Schiller is the chief exponent of this theory. Every individual possesses energy to

perform work and whatever is left after attending the daily work and duties, that is utilized in playing. But on several occasions, we find tired and weak children playing. In such cases, the theory is proved ineffective. Children generally remain dependent on their elders, and therefore, they possess much surplus energy. We find them playing most of the time during day and night.

2. *Recreative Theory:* Play is a recreational activity. School children and workers engaged in various jobs become tired after their work and that consumes much of their energy. It is through play that they regain their lost energy. Play is recreation and joy for them to refresh.
3. *Recapitulation Theory:* Stanley Hall is the originator of this theory. He believes that children play and they pass through the same stages of development through which their ancestors have passed. In the beginning of human civilization, man had the same mental development through which a young child passes today. Children inherit various traits of their ancestors and the same they recapitulate through the play.
4. *Anticipatory Theory:* Contrary to the belief that children play and pass through the stages of development of their ancestors, Karl Groos has observed that creatures play to prepare themselves for future life and vocation. Puppies play and quarrel and learn to fight because in future they know that they have to fight as dogs. Children play and act as doctors in their clinics, girls prepare small houses and dolls and perform scenes of marriage, some children run a shop and others play a role of railway guard, etc. In this way, children unconsciously prepare for their future life and vocation. They translate their imagination into play.
5. *Cathartic Theory:* Human beings are not completely free of their primitive mode of living. Many a time men exhibit, whenever an opportunity comes, their primitive traits, which generally remain subdued because of social bonds. According to the cathartic theory, the primitive modes of behaviour get an outlet for their expression in the form of play.

Summing up the theoretical discussion, it can be concluded that modern games like cricket, hockey, football and tennis are means of recreation. But this is also undeniable that man has definitely inherited some mental traits of past generations. Playing games is the source of our surplus energy and they prepare us for future life and vocations.

Play and Education

Karl Groos is of the opinion that play is experimental. Playing makes children and infants familiar with objects, develop in them the sense and trains their organs. They get experience of shape, colour, and functions of several objects. Children run about and chase one another during play, and these are exercises for their physical growth. Some games are of constructive nature and they train hands and develop mental skills. The teacher can motivate children to prepare models and useful articles. The tendency of inventive plays is stimulated by organizing 'science fairs' and exhibitions.

Playway in education reflects the tendency of constructiveness in children. Play is the symbol of an individual's nature and personality. A teacher can develop in students various qualities through play. Seriousness of the purpose can be developed through the activity of games and plays. It is through play that a teacher creates interest in learning various tactics which are useful for daily work. The entire environment of school can be made congenial. Freedom, responsibility, joy and cooperation can be infused in the character of pupils through the playway method of education. The playway method creates in the mind of students the difference between good and evil, interesting or uninteresting, just or unjust. Various techniques of play have been introduced by educationists such as kindergarten, montessori, project-method, heuristic method, Dalton plan, scouting, guiding, etc. These methods have made education interesting as well as constructive. It is no exaggeration that play develops in pupils virtues for a successful life and habits of being adjusted with various situations. Educational tours are the sources of lessons of History, Geography, Nature-Study, Civics, Economics and Sociology. There is left no knowledge of any subject which cannot be given through Scouting. Scouting and NCC are play-based activities in schools and colleges which develop in students self-independence, motives of self and voluntary services and social service, besides commitment for one's own country or nation. Playway education is considered as the primary source of teaching a democratic way of civic life.

QUESTIONS

Short Answer Type Questions

1. Define 'Powers of Mind'.
2. What are instincts?
3. What is reflex action?
4. What is imitation?
5. Define sympathy.
6. Define suggestions.
7. What do you mean by play as an innate tendency.

Average Answer Type Questions

1. Discuss 'Educational Value of Play'.
2. Describe 'Types of Suggestions'.
3. What is the educational significance of suggestions?
4. How does sympathy affect teaching in the classroom?
5. Discuss various types of Imitation and their impact on learning.

Essay Type Questions

1. Natural Tendencies of Child.
2. Inherent Powers of the Mind.
3. Instincts and their Educational a Significance.

References

Bernard, L.L., *A Study in Social Psychology*, Holt, NY, 1926.

Bridges, K.M.B., 'Emotional Development in Early Infancy', *Child Development*, Vol. 3, 1932.

Chaube, S.P., *Development Psychology*, L.N. Agarwal & Sons, Agra, 1986.

Crow, L.D. and A. Crow, *Educational Psychology*, Eurasia, New Delhi, 1964.

Bowley, A.H. et al., *Psychology: The Study of Man's Mind*, Odhams, London, 1949.

Freud, S., *The Problem of Anxiety*, Norton, NY, 1936.

Gates, A.I. et al., *Educational Psychology*, Barnes and Noble, NY, 1935.

Lindgren, H.C., *Educational Psychology in the Classroom*, Wiley, NY, 1972.

Mathur, S.S., *Educational Psychology*, Vinod Pustak Mandir, Agra, 1998.

McDougall, R.S., *Introduction to Social Psychology*, Methuen, London, 1944.

Piaget, J. and S. Inhalder, *The Psychology of the Child*, Routledge & Kegan Paul, London, 1969.

Sharma, R.A., *Technology of Teaching*, International Publishing House, Meerut, 1981.

Sharma, Yogendra K., *Textbook of Educational Psychology*, Kanishka, New Delhi, 2004.

Skimmer, C.E. (Ed.), *Educational Psychology*, Longmans, London.

Thurstone, L.L., *Primary Mental Abilities*, University of Chicago Press, Chicago, 1938.

Valentine, C.W., *Psychology and its Bearing on Education*, Methuen, London, 1957.

Woodworth, R.S. and D.G. Marquis, *Psychology*, Methuen, London, 1949.

Part II

Process of Human Growth and Development

4

Heredity and Environment

Impact on Pupils' Development

A child is born with inherited powers. These powers grow and develop in various stages of a child's life like infancy, childhood, adolescence, youth and maturity. These are also influenced by mental, physical and environmental conditions and have their impact on his daily activities. It is very relevant to discuss the bases of these powers' growth. Psychologists believe that development of the various powers of child is the product of his hereditary and environmental conditions.

Some people have the notion that whatever the child is, he or she is due to his or her parents. If the parents are good, their offsprings are also good; and if they are bad, their children too are of a bad nature. They are of the opinion that a child's basis of development lies in heredity. But this is incorrect, and you may come across dull children of bright parents, or bright children of dull parents. In fact, heredity is not the sole cause of the nature of a child's development. What then are the reasons for our being what we are? Is heredity responsible for our social, moral or intellectual development? Or, is it the environment in which the child grows? This is a complicated problem and none can be sure which of the two opinions are correct.

A teacher is very much concerned about the appropriate and positive development of pupils. He tries to understand the heredity of pupils, and at the same time provides the child a congenial environment through the school programmes. He believes that effects of heredity can be transformed and moral values can be inculcated through a healthy mode and devices of teaching.

In the present chapter, we shall try to understand how far environmental conditions are responsible for the development of children, and to what extent heredity is proved effective.

What is Heredity?

Life of an organism begins with the meeting of two germ cells. In the ovary of the female, an ovum is present. It is a kind of female's egg cell. It contains 23 very minute pairs of 46 chromosomes. In the male's sperm also are present 23 pairs of chromosomes. Fertilization takes place when chromosomes of male and female meet and life begins to take place. In this process of heredity, an individual gets traits from his parents. We may notice that chromosomes are the carriers of heredity. A child may have eyes like the father and fingers like the mother. There may also be a child who resembles neither father, nor mother. This happens because chromosomes have numerous genes and only these genes determine the traits to be inherited. The kind of contribution made, it depends on the nature of the genes of father and mother.

Heredity is not a matter only of father and mother's chromosomes where the genes of one of the two generally 'get hidden'. It is also a matter of the next generation in which the children may inherit the colour of eyes, shape of hair, complexion of the skin, etc., of ancestors. This means that characteristics in the offspring are not manifested by parents alone, they may be possessed by grandparents and even great-grandparents. Heredity is the result of the union of the genes.

Francis Galton made a statistical study of the transmission of various traits from generation to generation. Galton's Law states: "The two parents between them contribute on an average one-half of each inherited faculty, each of the grandparents controlling one-quarter of it; the four great-grandparents one-eighth, or each of great-grandparents one-sixteenth and so on, the sum of the series is equal to 1 or the total inheritance of the organism" (Figure 4.1).

Figure 4.1

Galton's Law of Heredity

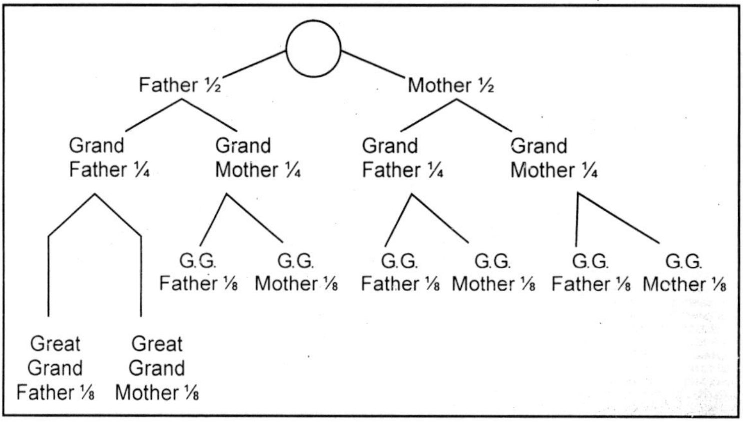

Gregor Mendel's view also finds a solution to the phenomenon of similarity and variations. He carried out a series of experiments on garden peas, and these were later extended to animals like mice, rats, rabbits, etc.

Mendel discarded the theory that when A and B meet, they give rise to $\frac{A+B}{2}$. He was of the opinion that traits in the new individual may be the dominant of the recessive traits of the parents. Mendel took two peas – one tall (TT) and the other short (SS). They were sown and cross-fertilized – dominant trait (TT) and shortness (SS) as the recessive one. The result of cross-fertilization may be understood by looking at the Figure 4.2.

It is clear from the figure that when tall and short peas are cross-fertilized, tall being the dominant trait, the result was tall peas having a recessive trait of shortness. Mendel got the tall and short peas in the ratio of 3:1 – the pure tall being one, impure tall two and the pure short one. Again, when pure talls were self-fertilized, they produced pure talls and so also by the self fertilization of pure shorts, these resulted pure short ones. Similarly, the tall and the short were again in the ratio of 3:1. It is clear that the recessive trait lies dominant in the offspring in the absence of the dominant, the chances of which are one in four; it comes to the forefront and become predominant.

Figure 4.2

Mendel Cross-Fertilization

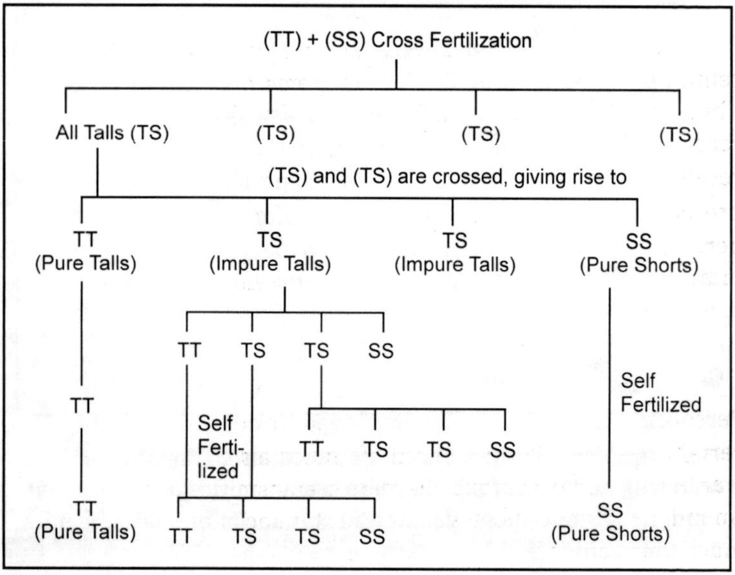

General Laws of Heredity

Heredity has three laws which affect the individual's personality:

(i) *Like begets like* states that the children have a tendency to be like their parents, i.e., like father or like mother or both in one way or the other. But it is not true in all cases and suffers from that of many variations like colour or even intelligence.

(ii) *Law of variation* states that children vary in many cases from their parents. This is because of the fact that the germ cells of the parents have genes which unite in various ways; and each combination produces a different quality of offspring.

(iii) *Law of regression* states that "the tendency for the children of very bright parents to be less bright than their parents, and comparable tendency for the children of very inferior parents to be less inferior, is called regression". The reason for regression is the union of the best traits of the father with the best traits of the mother. But in case of mating gifted with the opposite less gifted, the resulting offspring may be of inferior caliber. Likewise, the offspring of dull parents would be better, if the germ cells of the parents are better than the combination from which they have developed.

Heredity decides the physique of individual or organisms. Men cannot fly like birds, or fish cannot remain alive without water. Thus, the capabilities of individuals are within the limits of the received genes. Some of the individuals because of their genes received from heredity can learn new experiences which were not present in their ancestors. Galton, therefore, states that a child's heredity is received from his far and far-off ancestors, and an individual is not only the giver of birth, but he is also the preserver of germ cells.

Heredity and Personality

Personality traits are mostly developed through environment. But certain qualities are influenced by genes also. Anger of father or fear in mother may perhaps have been transmitted to the offspring. An individual inherits only genes but his social personality is very much the product of the environment and family traits.

Temperament is an important part of personality. But man's nature depends on environment and a difference in environment affects temperament. Experiments have proved that temperament is nothing to do with heredity, it is due to internal drives which are deeply affected by endocrine glands. Some scientists believe to the extent that glands determine personality. We may notice the change in boys and girls because of effects of sex glands.

Environment

What is environment? Environment is not simply our natural surroundings, but includes our family and neighbourhood relations. Thus, environment has two distinct categories – natural and social. Natural environment refers to all those things and forces that the earth around us constitutes.

The social environment of human beings is as old as civilization itself. Civilization is not an abstract notion, but what a person sees around himself on acquiring consciousness in the society, i.e., language, various arts, religion, constitution, means of communication, wealth, means of luxury, etc.

Whatever is around human beings, except their acquired genes, is given by environment. Its scope is very wide. The basic traits of human behaviour, of course, lie in heredity, but their form and functional development are decided by conditions of environment. Environmental conditions provide human beings with opportunities for acquiring new behavioural activities and vocations. Environment, in the aggregate, means all the intrinsic forces and conditions which affect the life, nature, behaviour, growth, development and maturation of living organisms.

An individual's activities and capacity to perform work are not inherited, but his functional power is inherited. Whether power will be functional or not, it depends on his environmental conditions. Heredity and social traditions and conditions are carriers of growth of an individual. Heredity provides force, and environment is responsible for making the force functional. A favourable environment may develop an individual in a positive direction. But this favourable advantage is limited to the individual, and it cannot be inherited from his ancestors.

Educational Significance of Heredity and Environment

Darwin's theory of 'survival of the fittest' cannot be taken as educationally adequate. The theory would imply that only intelligent children have the right to education, and dull, weak and backward children have no chances and opportunities to get an education. This theory is defunct because it creates divisions in society and negative competition, hate and envy would disrupt the right of democratic education. The right to education for all and to provide equal opportunities to all are the basic tenets of our democratic set-up.

It is not man himself who moulds his life according to environment, but he has the capacity and force to change the environmental conditions according to his needs and objectives of leading a good life. The aims of education are not to make a child helpless and worthless. Education has nobler objectives of developing a child as a useful citizen by revising and moulding environmental situations accordingly.

Education can make pupils adapt to their complex living condition. It can reform and change the attitude of pupils and make them civilized. The work of education is a continuous process, and is seeking newer grounds for each generation. McDougall, therefore, has the opinion that inherited values are developed step-by-step and with patience.

Each individual faces different types of responses from a similar environment. This is because of the fact that the genes of each pupil are not the same. It is also evident that even real brothers and sisters develop differences in likings, abilities and emotional susceptibilities despite being brought up in an apparently similar environment. A teacher's role is important in the sense that he should not diminish the tradition of heredity, rather he should make all efforts to utilize the innate tendencies of his pupils. Pupils having a low IQ cannot be changed by education easily. The teacher should utilize their innate qualities and provide adequate, healthy education as per their levels of intelligence. All possible opportunities should be provided to these children so that they may develop their capacities by a sequential process of education.

Social Environment and Education

A child takes birth with biological heredity but grows amidst social heritage, caste, culture, art, literature, traditions of society, etc., which are components of social environment. The values of a healthy social heritage may reduce vices and ill-effects of traditions in the same manner as a weak individual may be guarded by proper medical knowledge. Similarly, a healthy school environment may improve the weaknesses of pupils. This may be done by providing reinforced education by scientific methods and psychological attitude of the teacher and the taught. It is mostly the school and social environment which mould the pupils' behaviour for good. A child learns in the same manner as the human race is being developed by the process of knowledge and learning. In the light of the 'theory of recapitulation', the teacher may orient the teaching methodology by utilizing the child's social environment and social heritage. This may develop an interest in the child's learning process and education too may prove to be socially useful.

Literature and history may be taught through instances and stories from sources of culture and civilization with proper adhering to the principles of secularism. The teacher should take proper care and make use of the heuristic method, process of induction of educational principles, playway method, activity and project methods, Dalton plan, etc. These techniques create an environment that benefits children in the classroom.

QUESTIONS

Short Answer Type Questions

1. *Define:*
   - (a) Heredity
   - (b) Chromosomes
   - (c) Galton's Law
   - (d) Mendel Theory

Average Answer Type Questions

1. Discuss 'heredity and personality'.
2. What is environment?
3. Discuss the ways and means to utilize social environment for seeking goals of healthy education.
4. Discuss the relationship between heredity and education.
5. What are General laws of heredity?

Essay Type Questions

1. Heredity and Environment
2. Role of Environment on Child's Education
3. Impact of Heredity and Environment on Education
4. Social Environment and Education

References

Barron, F., *Creative Person and Creative Process*, Holt, NY, 1969.

Bernard, H.W., *Psychology of Learning and Teaching*, McGraw-Hill, NY, 1972.

Chaube, S.P., *Development Psychology*, L.N. Agarwal & Sons, Agra, 1986.

Crow, L.D. and A. Crow, *Educational Psychology*, Eurasia, New Delhi, 1964.

Jennings, H.H., *Genetics*, Norton, N.Y., 1935.

Lindgren, H.C., *Educational Psychology in the Classroom*, John Wiley, NY, 1956.

Mathur, S.S., *Educational Psychology*, Vinod Pustak Mandir, Agra, 1981.

Simpson, R.H., *Improving Teaching Learning Process*, Longmans, NY, 1953.

Sorenson, H., *Psychology and Education*, McGraw-Hill, NY, 1938.

Tyler, L.E., *The Psychology of Human Differences*, Appleton, NY, 1956.

Verma, I.B., *Fundamentals of Education Psychology*, Sri Ram Mehra, Agra, 1951.

5

Human Growth and Development

Physical and Motor Development

Physical Development

Beginning of Life

Life begins and the human foetus appears as a tiny blob of protoplasm. In a month, the blob takes the shape of 'embryo' and in the second month it becomes a foetus. After nearly five months, the mother feels the movement of foetus. Gradually, the growth follows from head to feet. There is a rapid growth of life in the first year and the male child is usually taller than the female. Rapid growth continues up to the third year. After it, the growth becomes slow.

Boys and girls vary in both height and weight. W.M. Krogman gives data of height and weight of children of a California school of age group 5–15 years as under:

Table 5.1

Height-Weight Variation: Boys and Girls (Age: 5–15)

Age	*Range in Height (inches)*		*Range in Weight (kgs)*	
	Boys	*Girls*	*Boys*	*Girls*
5	39.47	39.47	34.53	33.53
6	39.50	39.50	34.63	33.63
7	41.53	41.53	37.73	36.73
8	42.55	41.55	39.78	38.81
9	44.58	45.57	42.91	43.89
10	47.60	46.50	48.101	45.105
11	48.63	48.62	50.117	49.120
12	50.65	50.65	55.128	56.137
13	52.67	53.67	60.142	62.151
14	54.67	55.67	66.146	70.152
15	56.67	56.67	74.148	82.153

As reflected in the table, an average girl will be taller than an average boy. The rate of growth of each child is different. The weight of the child is largely dependent on height rather than age. One who is taller must be heavier in weight.

Physical Changes in Childhood

Physical changes influence the child's interest, and also his or her activities. Psychologically the child becomes aware of being small or big before the big-ones or small-ones. This awareness influences the behaviour of a child to a great extent. Elder members in the family often tell a child, "You are a big boy or girl now, behave decently and do not be childish".

Physical changes by size and age also affect maturing of the brain and the whole nervous system. Increase in height and weight also affect the size of the head. It does not increase in size proportionately. A six-year-old child has generally 90 per cent of an adult's head size, and at 12 years age, it is only 95 per cent. Various organs of the body increase by age, but the increase is uneven in relation to other parts.

Bones and muscles of a child are flexible, soft and can be bent easily, whereas in an adult's case, these are liable to be broken by bending. The teacher in lower classes, therefore, instructs children to sit erect. He always remains careful about their right postures. The weight of a child's muscles, power and activity grow in coordination gradually.

A teacher should not expect a child to be able to solve complex problems because his level of mental maturity is lower than an adult. This development and physical changes affect the course of learning and techniques of teaching. It is necessary that to maintain physical balance of a child, he or she must be given physical training during the first 10 years of the life of the child. There must be a period of physical education in the time-table for pupils up to class VIII. In primary and junior classes, full care should be given to nutrition, physical health, play and exercise. During adolescence also, some sort of physical training - such as scouting, NCC, hiking and other out-door activities, including games of various types - should be arranged in their regular courses of education.

Physical Changes in Adolescence

It is a very critical period and generally it is reckoned from 12 to 18 years of age in our country. It is the period when the boy's sex glands are able to discharge sperms and can fertilize the female ovum. In our country, usually the girl's age of puberty is 12 or 13 years and in boys it is 13 or 14 years. The period of adolescence shows dramatic bodily changes. In girls, menstruation starts taking place, and the boys acquire manly traits and they are capable of sexual discharge. Adolescents gain much weight, the voice becomes deeper. The girls' breasts appear and their rounding off takes place. These changes embarrass the children and they develop certain tendencies of self-centrism. Some mature earlier, while others are physically younger. They behave awkwardly and sometimes become a problem for the teacher. Handling adolescent students can be a real test for a teacher. They develop certain bad tendencies. Their physical appearance and characteristics create misunderstandings for the teacher. The teacher should be very careful about the capabilities of such children. The outward appearance should not be the index of their character.

Motor Development

Meaning

Motor development of a child is significant in the same sense that it is related to strength, speed, precision and skill in the use of arms, legs and other parts of body muscles. Motor development makes a child learn to adapt himself with social and environmental situations. A child's emotional and mental behaviour are to some extent affected by his or her motor activities. Intellectual curiosity is satisfied through motor activities because these are concerned with proper handling and manipulating situations. The joy of success depends much on the child's capabilities in applying his or her motor activities.

Development during Pregnancy

Development during pregnancy is divided into two parts: (a) motor development, and (b) sensory development.

(a) *Motor development*: During pregnancy, the embryo shows before the birth movement, felt by the pregnant woman carrying the child. The beating of heart starts at the age of three weeks and after 18 weeks, it becomes audible. Children born in the sixth month of pregnancy produce certain sounds.
(b) *Sensory development* is also a part of motor development. The embryo in the eighth week becomes susceptible to epidermic sensations. It begins to react to pressure and temperature.

Growth

The bodily parts develop gradually in the child during pregnancy. After the birth, during the one to nine months, the eyes, hands, back and figures attain expertise, and movement of legs and feet is evident. At the age of a year-and-a-half, bubbling sounds are produced, and at the age of three, the child develops the capacity for thought and reasoning. Later, his socialization begins and at the age of five, he or she moves in the company of children in the family and the neighbourhood.

Steps of Development

The development passes through various stages. Rousseau has determined the four major stages in the development as: (i) infancy, (ii) childhood, (iii) adolescence, and (iv) adulthood. Infancy lasts generally till six year from birth, childhood from 6 to 12 and adolescence from 12 to 18.

Motor Activities during Infancy Period

Motor development of an infant passes through sequential stages like gripping or holding objects, sitting with some assistance, playing with objects, standing with some help, standing holding furniture, wall, etc., moving on knees, standing on own, walking, climbing, standing alone.

Factors Promoting Motor Development

Adequate freedom should be provided to the child and indirect supervision must be given for development of motor skill. The child needs open space to play and move around using limbs and various parts of the body. He should be given simple and easy exercises to make him learn to control his head, shoulders, hips and the upper part. Motor development leads to learning, and it should be introduced in schools and colleges through physical education and games. Proper assistance should also be provided to give pupils training in handicrafts, carpentry and woodwork. Manual training should be provided up to class VIII .

Teacher's Role

It is very essential for a teacher to have a knowledge of effective methods promoting ways and means of achieving the skill. Only then can the teacher transmit successfully the motor jobs and can win the admiration and confidence of pupils. The teacher must be careful that attainment of the skill for children should not become a tardy job. Encouragement must be given to children even for their unrefined performances. A situation must not be allowed to create bleakness for the training of the skill. It is, therefore, for the class teacher to foresee this situation or contingency and prevent it by continuously giving encouragement and sympathy. A stage or curve of 'plateau of learning' should be discovered by the teacher, and he should contrive to remove it through changing the techniques of teaching methodology.

During the course of providing training, the teacher should be careful to avoid critical comments for incomplete or undone tasks. These may have an adverse effect and a situation may arise when the affected student may become despondent and discouraged, as much as to think of leaving the task. Therefore, the student should be sympathetically set on proper lines by adequate guidance and encouragement. The learner should be given a proper activity which may help him remove the hindrances.

Involvement of Pupils

The main cause of failure in motor skill is following wrong actions or tracks by students. The teacher may himself demonstrate to the students and involve them in continuous practice in the performance of the activity. Constant repetition of the job is not enough. This would not help to generate motor skill in students. It is most desirable to involve students in their state of complete mental consciousness. The practice must be mentally attended to. The learner of the motor skill should be aware of the objective, and should be constantly made conscious about the same. The teacher should evaluate the learners during the course of the process in terms of the desired objective of the job. The teacher can produce very skilled workers of motor activities provided he pays individual attention to each student.

Speed and Exactness: Practice and Individual Differences

Motor skill and the associated work cannot be successfully done hurriedly. In the beginning, pupils should be directed to go slowly and steadily but avoiding faults and mistakes. Gradually, the students may be encouraged to improve speed. Once the pupil learns and the correct habit is formed, the motor activity becomes quite automatic. Constant practice should be mentally attended to. But when a person becomes habitual of it, he does not require constant repetition. If a person has learnt his typing well, he can pick up speed unconsciously.

Proper and adequate practice with an aim is essential for gaining progress, speed and correct performance of the job. Motor skill differs from person to person because the problems, capabilities and abilities of each individual differ. The teacher should, therefore, take into consideration the individual traits or characteristics of students.

QUESTIONS

Short Answer Type Questions

1. *Define:*
   (a) Embryo and foetus
   (b) Size of head of male and female child
   (c) Bones and muscles of a child
   (d) Physical education
   (e) Physical changes at age 12
   (f) Motor development
2. *State against the following statements: 'R' for right and 'W' for wrong:*
   (a) Boys and girls grow evenly in their weight and height.
   (b) Bones of a child can be bent easily.
   (c) Organs of body increase by age unevenly.
   (d) Physical training is not necessary in primary schools.

Average Answer Type Questions

1. Discuss physical changes during adolescence.
2. 'Motor development during pregnancy'. Discuss briefly.
3. What are the factors promoting motor development?
4. What are the stages of development and their age limit?

Essay Type Questions

1. Role of teachers promoting motor skill in pupils.
2. Physical changes during childhood (5 to 10 years).
3. Education and the physique of the child.

References

Gesell, A.L. and F.H. Ilg, *The Child from Five to Ten*, Harper, NY, 1946.

Goodenough, F.L. and C.R. Brain, 'Certain Factors Underlying the Acquisition of Motor Skills by Preschool Children', *Journal of Experimental Psychology*, Vol. 1, 1916.

Hurlock, F.B., *Child Development*, McGraw-Hill, NY, 1942.

Krogman, W.M., "A Handbook of the Measurement and Interpretation of Height and Weight in the Growing Child" (Society for Research in the Child Development) 48: 41, Table: XIII, quoted from Mathur, S.S., *Educational Psychology*, Vinod Pustak Mandir, Agra, 1981.

Mathur, S.S., *Educational Psychology*, Vinod Pustak Mandir, Agra, 1998.

Sharma, Yogendra K., *Textbook of Educational Psychology*, Kanishka, New Delhi, 2004.

Sorenson, H., *Psychology in Education*, McGraw-Hill, NY, 1948.

Verma, I.B., *Fundamentals of Educational Psychology*, Sri Ram Mehra, Agra, 1952.

6

Social and Cultural Development

Social growth means the increasing ability of an individual to mix and work with others conveniently, comfortably and with joy and happiness. H. Sorenson defines social growth as "the increasing ability to get along with oneself and others". A newly-born child is neutral as far as the tendency of mixing up with others. A child likes to get along happily in the lap of his mother. But as he grows in age, he or she begins to become social and starts to get along with others. In the family, he begins to move with other members of his age or with elders, knowing that they meet his demands and fulfil his needs. He feels satisfied with family members who give him love and help him to get along comfortably. He also begins to act according to the norms of the family. He begins to understand that to meet his daily requirements, it is necessary to follow the path as suggested by the elders of the family. He also makes necessary changes in his inborn tendencies, attitude and behaviour. In this way, he learns to react positively against others.

In the family and also in the neighbourhood, the child with growing age learns to adjust by following the norms of society. In other words, it can be said that children by and by learn to make adjustments and attain social behaviour. Their interests also are changed to adjust adequately according to the social environment. This is called the process of socialization. The process of social growth is the progressive improvement in an individual by understanding the social heritage of his own group, i.e., the traditions and customs, and also moulding his conduct to a reasonable conformity with this heritage.

Socialization is the process of leading one's personality from a general and simple behaviour to a social behaviour of complex nature, conforming to special interests, feelings, ideals and culture. This means a change in the understanding of an individual to accept cultural shift for reacting positively to the pattern of individual aspirations. In the words of F.F. Powers, "the individual's social circumstances are constantly undergoing change, and the individual must perforce change with these circumstances". This process is known as the development of socialization.

Stages of Social Maturity

The beginning of social development for an infant or a young child is the mother. She forms his immediate environment and feeds him. The child feels happy in his mother's company. As he grows, the entire family becomes his environment where the child reacts and makes adjustment to each of the members and his physical pleasure is changed to mental satisfaction. During infancy, his activities show that he has started understanding the objects and generally becomes ego-centric and selfish. He does not allow to give up his possessions to anyone else. At the age of one, the child begins to come into contact with other children of the same age group. But he remains interested in the company of elders because they satisfy his needs. He becomes the attraction of elders. From the age of two to five years, he plays with his fellow beings and feels happy in their company. Sometimes he feels annoyed and quarrels for objects and is satisfied only when his needs are met by elders in the family.

In the company of children of the age group of four to five, the child begins to develop 'self'. This is the stage when children develop consciousness of their success and failure. Many times they do not follow the wishes of elders and oppose their instructions. This is the period when their capacity of judging and adhering to suggestions of others is developed. Through many playway activities, children imitate and put themselves in positions of others. The child acts as a doctor, railway guard, sometimes acts like a horse, an engine, cop, etc. The motive is to gain friendship of other children. Thus, the social behaviour of children goes through rapid changes and the status of personality begins to attain sociability. He begins to identify himself as one of the members of his own society and his attachment with the social norms and ideals becomes gradually stronger.

Children with their entry into school and at the age of about 10 grow highly social and develop friendly relations with a small group of classmates of their tastes and interests. Gradually, their social relations are developed and their activities are organized as well as competitive. But this may not be the universal phenomenon and many boys prefer to remain individualistic. Participation of boys and girls is equally evident but generally the social customs allow only companionship with their own sex.

Influence of Culture

Customs and culture of the country where the children are born affect their sociability a lot. Social behaviour of children of our country differs to a great extent from the countries of the West and Middle East. In our country, mixing with people is uncommon and is governed by caste, religion, sex and regionalism. Economic status of families too is a common factor which governs the social relationship. Children born in poor families mix up with the children of their own economic status. They develop consciousness of being inferior in a way and hesitate in playing with the children of privileged class. Their social dealings too, at times, reflect the divide.

The teacher often faces critical situations in the class because of presence of pupils of privileged class and children from poor families. Both should be dealt with utmost care, sympathy and by providing even resources for adequate social behaviour. The teacher should approach them with an unbiased attitude but with a different outlook so that none of the two contradictory groups are hurt psychologically. It is necessary to judge them from the angle of bringing them at par with respect to their individuality and the objectives which are to be achieved.

Psychological Bases of Social Behaviour

In the development of social behaviour, several factors work for its positive integration. Some of these are basic and have a direct influence. These are:

Sympathy

For the good of society and for adequate development of individuality, sympathy plays a significant role. Suggestion is the mental process in which the thought of one individual influences and moulds those of others. Suggestion is a form of symbol and this can be communicated by words and, pictures. A child follows the suggestion provided by the teacher in the class. It finds acceptance among children of the class even if it is not logical. Word suggestion is used by the teacher to complete the mental process or ideas. It is also used to indicate the effect of some stimuli on children's-mind. The teacher's temperament, age and experience and intellectual ability play an important role in making his suggestion.

Suggestion influences the child's behaviour with others as well as one's own behaviour. There are some students in the class who are conversely affected by suggestion, and they act in contradiction to the suggestion that is conveyed to them. The teacher may use various means and methods to make the suggestion effective. Ideo-motor suggestion engages students in action immediately. The teacher gives no time to think or discuss. For example, a teacher may ask pupils to draw a line parallel to the base of a triangle and passing through the vertex. Pupils accept the advice of a teacher who is considered to be a specialist. It is known as a prestige suggestion. The prestige suggestion has its influence everywhere. Students accept sayings of learned scholars like Radhakrishnan, Tagore, Mahatma Gandhi, Socrates, Plato and Aristotle without further preamble.

Friendship and Cooperation

In the classroom, children generally develop a group of friends who cooperate with each other in their social behaviour and activities. It is a psychological fact that children support the choice of their friends and cooperate with them. Sociability increases because of friendship in a profession, business, nearness of place, etc. Psychologically, common social motives, friendship and cooperation depend primarily on similar thinking ideas, and also on similar interests. People are much more social when they meet fellow partners having similar objectives.

Competition

Tendency for competition varies with increased interests. When the child gradually becomes mature, there is a competitive attitude shift in domestic functions. He observes parents, and also his brothers and sisters. His attention and interests also keep him alert to function better than others. He takes guard for his safety, and also becomes careful about the love of others towards him. When the child becomes conscious about his needs and takes care about the fear of their non-fulfilment, he reacts with anger, and with sorrow. This reaction gives in his mind a sort of competition to protect his self-motives against other fellows. As a doer of any social business, the child shows an eagerness to go ahead of others. The competitive tendency arises with respect to physical force, self-respect and intelligence. In the school and classroom, children are found to move ahead of each other and they remain keen about their own individual respect than the respect of the group. Teachers also generate a feeling of competition among pupils to reinforce by awards in debates, etc., and also by giving prizes to show the best results in examinations.

Competition for undesirable activities is harmful because it is almost a waste of time, energy and against the objective of learning. But a competitive spirit for best writing, oratory, performance in games, quizzes and recitation of poems, etc., encourages excelling and success. Competition should be encouraged for creative activities and constructive work. Each child should get an opportunity to show his or her worth according to their maximum capacity and capabilities. But it is a special tendency and should not be open for common and routine class work. Competition should be discouraged if it destroys social relations. This will be a bad tendency if a cold war begins among players after a game. In the school, too, students should not be encouraged if competition among them generates jealousy and indecent behaviour.

Conditions Influencing Social Behaviour

Effect of Age and Health

Social dealings develop with age. But the development is affected by health. Having a healthy body promotes social relations. During childhood, if the children remain affected by ill-health, their development is not at par as compared to the children of good health. The child becomes peevish and selfish if he is attended with great caution and untimely love only because he is not keeping good health. The child with poor health and who is lean and thin suffers from an inferiority complex. He is not favourably treated by classmates. They tease and trouble him off and on and the social relations become distorted.

Effect of Family

It is a psychological fact that the eldest child in a family gets immense opportunities for social development. He gets love, sympathy and resources without any hindrance of all the members of the family. But as soon as other sons and daughters appear, the attention of family members is divided. The youngest child gets most of the opportunities of social development.

The character, attitude, economic status and social prestige of parents, as well as the love of family members have a distinct influence upon the social growth and behaviour of children.

Effect of Materials and Means of Amusement

Material resources of play and games as well as means of amusement affect social development. These means provide opportunities for mixing with various children. They come to know each other's traits, habits and attitudes. During this process of their being regularly mixing and adjusting with the situations, their social development takes place.

Effect of School

The agency of education is a significant place where children get several opportunities of social development. In a school, several types of persons are present. Teacher, principal, physical instructor, laboratory incharge and other subordinate staff come into contact with children. Besides these, several types of students mix up daily on various occasions like functions, celebrations, meetings and lectures of renowned personalities. These activities provide newer experiences to the school students. The behaviour and character of classmates also affect constantly. The books, methods of teaching and guidance of councillors, have their effects on the social growth and development of children during the school years. There are several occasions and opportunities when children display sympathy, cooperation, competition, friendliness, etc. The influences of their friends and neutrals as well as their opponents play an important role in the social development.

Effects of Society and its Traditions

Man is a social being. There are different types of social institutions in the country. People come into their contact on several occasions. They are born as a member of a particular society having its typical ideals, norms, traditions, culture, etc. These social norms are mild, flexible and positive in nature. Some of the traditions are fundamentally full of vices. Thus, a child being a member of the society learns some good and some bad traits. The role of education and teachers is to protect children and check or keep them away from vices through school activities, methods of teaching and disciplinary actions.

Social Development and Education

Education is the prime instrument contributing much in every stage of a child's social development. The role of lectures and books is limited in a way to mould social behaviour. It is the direct function of extra-curricular (now, co-curricular) programmes, the school's atmosphere, rules of conduct and discipline in the school, radio, cinema, newspapers and magazines, etc., to mould social behaviour. Group camps, picnics, hikes and tours, etc., have a healthy influence upon the individual's social development and socialization.

Educational programmes help in the development of character and qualities for social good. School children acquire good habits and some of them develop the qualities of leadership. Education is meant to provide pupils with opportunities for development of many kinds of skills which make them fit for the social good and becoming committed citizens of the country. The outdoor programmes in the school provide pupils with an informal atmosphere and freedom for mixing and meeting various sorts of people. They meet rich and poor, healthy and sick, good or bad, physically valid and invalid, people of various qualities. It helps the school children to learn to adjust in all sorts of critical situations and their social education is set in motion. It is very essential for teachers and parents to cooperate and provide adequate facilities and opportunities for healthy social growth to their wards.

Concluding the discussion it may be stated that a child grows and develops physically, mentally and emotionally to display a positive social behaviour. The process of social development goes incessantly through the stages of infancy, childhood and adolescence. Social growth means that the child becomes capable to adjust himself continually to an environment of social activities. The child gradually becomes mature and successfully develops awareness of others. He starts mixing with various types of people during the school days and also during his career later. The teacher should take care because individual behaviour differs. Some boys show behaviour of withdrawal and they should be motivated sympathetically so that they may mix with others without being shy. Some children are socially active and can adjust themselves in varying situations. Teachers should make it a point to bring about a right type of social adjustment by providing proper atmosphere in the classroom for evasive children or mischief-mongers, those who are aggressive and quarrelsome. The role of the teacher, however, should neither be autocratic, nor submissive. Complete social development is the motive for a teacher and he must work towards this with the cooperation of pupils, parents and other teachers as well.

QUESTIONS

Short Answer Type Questions

1. *Define:*

   (a) Social growth

   (b) Socialization

   (c) Social behaviour during infancy

(d) Stages of social maturity

(e) Cultural influences

(f) Social growth and sympathy

(g) Competition and social development

Average Answer Type Questions

1. What are the conditions for a child's social growth in the family? Describe briefly.
2. How does school play a role in the development of social behaviour?
3. What are traditions? How do they affect social behaviour?

Essay Type Questions

1. Social development process.
2. Favourable conditions promoting social growth of a child.
3. Education and social development.
4. Teacher's responsibilities in the development of social behaviour.

References

Anderson, J.E., *The Psychology of Development and Personal Adjustment*, Henry Holt, NY, 1949.

Mathur, S.S., *Educational Psychology*, Vinod Pustak Mandir, Agra, 1998.

Murphy, L.B., *Social Behaviour and Child Personality*, Columbia University Press, NY, 1937.

Sorenson, H., *Psychology in Education*, McGraw-Hill, NY, 1948.

Symonds, P.M., *Dynamics of Human Adjustment*, Appleton-Century, NY, 1946.

Verma, I.B. and Verma, L.N., *Fundamentals of Educational Psychology*, Sri Ram Mehra, Agra, 1954.

7

Mental Development

An individual's behaviour is not mechanical. He behaves and acts with some objective, or his actions are purposive. His innate powers are helpful in having mental experiences. The process of mental growth, however, is not a simple matter, it is quite a complex affair. Broadly, it includes the abilities in memory, imagination, language, precepts, concepts and problem-solving ability. The mental abilities can be measured by intelligence tests.

In the classroom, the teacher uses various devices and teaching methods. His objective is to guide and assist the child in the development of mental powers so that he can gain adequate knowledge and experience to reach a decision.

Role of Family in the Mental Development of a Child

The level of a child's mental powers and abilities is generally promoted initially in the social circumstances. This includes the influence of family, neighbourhood and school environment. In the family, if the atmosphere is favourable and the members are intellectually sound, naturally this may speed up the mental development of the child. Parents may create materials and the environment to satisfy the child psychologically. Each query of the child should be sympathetically met with and be reasonably satisfied. The child may also be provided with objects and sources to help him in solving quizzes, maze-exercises and incomplete stories, pictures to complete. Possession of radio, TV, and other scientific toys to promote thinking and understanding the problems help him to pick up certain intricacies and their proper solution.

Mother's influence generally is proved vital. Her care and guidance have produced the world's greatest saints, scientists, leaders and thinkers. The relations among family members must be amicably and healthily treated so that the young children do not live in a tense atmosphere. This also affects the mental growth of a child. The economic status and cultural level of the family affect the mental growth of children.

Neighbourhood and Child's Mental Growth

As soon as a child attains the school-going age, he goes out and mixes up with children in the neighbourhood. He develops intimacy with the environment of his locality and becomes familiar with the various elements comprising the natural and human world of the vicinity. The geography of neighbourhood exerts an important influence on his mental development.

There is also the possibility of picking up bad habits from the company of undesirable, troublesome and mischievous group of fellows in the neighbourhood. The parents and guardians of the child should keep a close watch on the friend circle and the child's activities and movements. If there is any problem, it may be treated sympathetically without using undue force.

Sequential Growth of Mental Domain

A child's mental domain develops gradually. He becomes familiar with the notion of time and distance. In the beginning, his attention is restricted to objects and matters or phenomena which are near and taking shape in front of him. He does not react to those phenomena which take place elsewhere and are far from his power of observation. With the development of age, he gradually grows. He begins to take cognition and reacts to the far and distant phenomena. Naturally, his sphere of knowledge widens to include the past and future.

Gradually, the pupil in the wider world of environment comes across symbolic knowledge. He begins to understand the elements in their real sense. In the beginning, he reacts against the complete stimulus, but with the development of mental power he is capable of reacting against a minor sign or symbol of stimulus.

By and by, the mental power of the individual goes on developing and he becomes richer in experience and intelligence. He can now plan his future activities in the hope of achieving fruitful results. He does not use only symbols for concrete actions but also moves towards abstract ideas.

The changes in mental power take place not abruptly but in stages. This means that the behaviour of an individual differs from stage to stage. During infancy it was different, and in the stages onward like childhood, adolescence and adulthood, the individual behaves altogether differently.

In the initial stage, a child's sensory functions are powerful. His cognition is characterized by touch, taste, etc. But after two-three years, he makes typical sounds and yells. After some more years, the child develops the capacity and power of imagination as obviously seen in the various games and play activities.

At the age of four to five years, children become inquisitive. They generally put forth several questions to elders. Their curiosity gets increased and they try to know about various phenomena of nature and also daily activities. There is contiguity in the development of a child's cognition. But there is a lot of difference in the development of power of cognition because of mental variations in individuals. This is evident in the form of varying types of behaviour of individuals and also different types of reaction in the relevant situation or phenomenon.

Cognitive Behaviour due to School Environment

After home and neighbourhood, the child's field is shifted to school education. School training has a potent influence in the development of mental power of children. They become emotionally invigorated to a chain of influences generated by the building and campus of the school, conduct of his teacher team, the curriculum followed, and methods of teaching in the classroom, the behaviour of classmates and also of senior class fellows and the administration and commandments of the discipline of the school. The daily impact of all the programmes in the school have their role in the cognitive development of pupils.

During infancy, a child's curiosity must be satisfied by the teacher. The teacher arouses the interest of a child in the subject which he is to teach, and then guide him to understand the main concepts of the lesson. A child may ask several questions about the main ideas involved in the lesson. A teacher must satisfy the child's query by all means without reproach. During the period of infancy, the teacher should use modern methods and should take help of technology like radio, television, film-strips, CDs, overhead projector, etc. These invariably affect the mental process and generate intellectual power. Programmes outside the classroom like visits to museums, biological parks, exhibitions, historic monuments, etc., increase the child's knowledge and understanding.

Children in the age group 6–12 are generally rich in their experiences because their mental cells are developed and they gain much from varied and complex environmental situations. The characteristic of gregariousness becomes intense and they prefer to mix up more with children of their own age. Team spirit and participation in games generate competition, which indirectly gives birth to cognitive behaviour. Children now do not get satisfied with the question-answer format but they remain anxious to be a part and parcel of their varied and complex environment. As members of a team, they become aware of moral norms and prefer taking interest in the good of team members rather than becoming aware of social values like right or wrong, just or unjust, true or false, real or unreal, etc. Children develop a possessive nature, creativity and imitation. They yearn for praise but are also pained when scolded or being pointed out.

The period between 12 and 18 years is known as the period of adolescence. It means that a growing boy or girl now has made a transition from childhood to maturity. The main characteristic of the adolescent period in life is that the children now move towards adulthood. They become more stable in their tendencies, habits and activities. Mental characteristics of the period of adolescence include developed mental abilities, sexual development, hero worship, religiosity, gregariousness, sentimentality, excessive imagination and development of particular traits or interests.

Piaget and Cognitive Development

Jean Piaget has pointed out four stages of development – the sensory period, pre-operational stage, concrete operational and formal operational stages. The sensory period belongs to infancy and it begins from birth and lasts for nearly 18 months. It is the period during which the child satisfies his physical wants. But the child remains confused regarding himself and his environment. He comprehends casually. His mental development is no more than that of an intelligent animal.

During the pre-occupational stage, which lasts till about seven years, the child can represent events through symbols and language. He can solve problems based on concrete items that are visible. His cognition is not clear and is limited. He is unable to understand others. He remains ego-centric.

The concrete operational stage (7–11 years) is the period when children recognize the basic attributes of objects. The child becomes familiar with number, weight, etc., and starts control over perception. He communicates with others and begins to understand their point of view also. He can also decide about ideas and whether to follow others or not. This stage is considered favourable in the sense of cooperation and healthy competition.

Figure 7.1

Piaget's Cognitive Behaviour in Life Stages

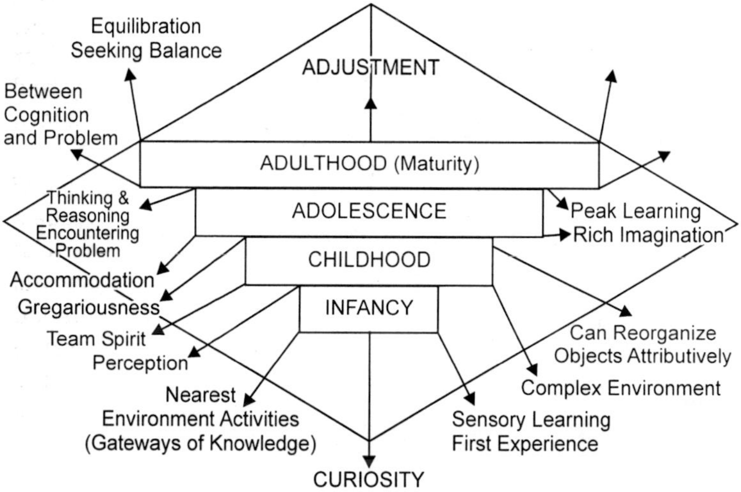

The stage of formal operation (from 12 to adolescence) is the period when the child possesses the ability of thinking and reasoning about phenomena of far and wide. He can solve problems systematically. The child now becomes able to reason out thinking and justifies his solution. He becomes intelligent to interact for the social good. Adolescents develop a logical attitude, but not necessarily realistic. They talk much of idealism and are radicals. But later on, during adulthood, there is developed an attitude of seeking balance.

Classroom Application of Piaget's Ideas

A teacher should understand very well how his pupils organize and synthesize ideas. He must be aware about their level of thinking and provide them with opportunities to perform experiments and listen to them patiently and know adequately their reactions. Let the pupils learn on their own. The teacher may form appropriate groups to facilitate social interaction. The groups should be of mixed type in which both advanced and less advanced pupils are placed. It facilitates learning from various sorts of ideas and thoughts received from different levels of pupils. The teacher should distinguish between concrete and formal suggestions provided by his pupils. He can ask each of the pupils on how they arrived at solutions to problems. The process of questioning may clear the validity of the situation under consideration. Pupils must be guided so that they may be more systematic to arrive at solutions of the problems. The entire process may develop a level of thinking scientifically and it may also raise the standard of pupils' cognition. Piaget's views actually make pupils understand the environment interactively. According to his theory, a child becomes sufficiently proficient in constructing schemes which are mentally sound to enable him to understand and deal successfully with his environment. Piaget's theory is of great value in classroom teaching provided the teacher himself is proficient enough with Piaget's schemes. It is essential for the teachers to know how their pupils organize and systematize ideas. This ultimately makes the process natural and easy. Teachers should be there with students to guide them.

Mental Development and Education

Growth of mental ability fosters such values in the child as truth, honesty, justice, obedience, discipline, cooperation, etc. The role of a teacher is to inculcate and strengthen these by setting adequate examples. The gregarious instinct in the child may induce group activities like scouting, excursions, field trips, and team games. Consequently, these can help the development of qualities like cooperation, fellow feeling, humanity, leadership, organization, patriotic feeling, social adjustment, readiness for help and performance of providing assistance, etc. Thus, mental development is an essential means for the development of a faithful citizen. Co-curricular activities are now considered an important part of education which have their source in mental development. These make the job of the teacher smooth and the behaviour of pupils is also transformed into the personality required for social good.

Process of Development of Various Mental Faculties

Processes of development of various mental faculties are important to understand. The various faculties have their educative values, and therefore the teacher should use these to mould the pupils' behaviour. The various faculties of mental development include sensation and perception, observation, attention and interest, memory, thinking and reasoning, imagination, learning and habit.

Sensation and Perception

A child during infancy gains knowledge through his sensory organs. Our eyes, ears, nose, tongue, skin, etc., are sensory organs. We get knowledge of external stimuli through these sensory organs. Thus, sensation is a reaction aroused in us by stimulus. It can be defined as an act of the sense organ which when stimulated, sends nerve currents to the sensory centres of the brain and the first response of the brain is sensation. We see a flower in the garden. But after a moment, we begin to analyse it and have knowledge that it is pink in colour. Seeing the flower is a pure sensation but the moment we begin to analyse its qualities and have knowledge that it is pink and gives a smell, it has petals, stem, etc., the sensation disappears and gives place to perception. Therefore, it can be concluded that the first response to a stimulus is sensation and perception is the next response of the organism following a sensation. R.S. Woodworth, thus, defines that in perception, "the chain of the events is: stimulus, response of the sense organ and sensory nerve, first cortical response, which is sensation, and second cortical response which is perception".

Sensory organs are called the gateways of knowledge and children get their first experience through their various senses. Therefore, Montessori's methods of education during infancy are based on sense training. At the kindergarten stage, the child learns the use of vision by playing with balls of different colours and forms. Auditory training is given by different types of mechanical toys producing different types of sounds. The child generally can learn to distinguish between the voices of animals. Auditory training is necessary for the development of correct pronunciations of words. In Montessori schools, the child is provided with pieces of different types of cloth such as muslin, silk, woollen, synthetic and non-synthetic, etc. These make him learn different types of touch.

The main technique of training a sense organ is to provide suitable stimuli to the child.

Perception is the basis of all human activities and mental processes. Accurate perception is to be got only when an individual is free from emotional difficulties and also from prejudices or biases. It is a well-organized process. The change in our environment attracts our attention and compels us to perceive phenomena. Every moment we come into contact with various stimuli but we are generally attracted to some specific stimuli at a time and our sensory organs respond to them.

We attend to an object or we prefer to perceive when something is novel, i.e., moving or making a sound or creating something. Its influence on our mind is intense. New scenes and novel sounds appear move attractive and strike our mind. If a teacher in the class presents a novel idea through charts or diagrams, the children become attentive to catch it. Similarly, in case an idea is repeated again and again in the class, children react positively towards it and understand its significance. They are attracted and perceive or get perception under several conditions like change in environment, intensity of stimulus, novelty, repetition, motivation, etc. The teacher in the class, therefore, recapitulates concepts with his questions to make them understand.

Motivation by the teacher in a classroom attracts the attention of even a dullard or backward child. He begins to take interest and tries to perceive the chart, model or experiment demonstrated by the teacher. Motivation removes difficulties and makes pupils alert to perceive stimulus related to their understanding of facts and knowledge.

Gestalt View of Perception

According to Gestalt, perception of an object should be in its completeness or in its whole form. The mental development through various sense organs is incomplete so long as it is not assimilated to the 'whole' of the object. Perception is useful only when a child perceives the whole body. If the child goes on to recognize the object through various sensory organs, there is the possibility of misunderstanding the reality. In education and classroom teaching, the teacher must begin with a complete sense or synoptic view of the lesson, and later on its details may be given. He, therefore, follows the dictum: "Proceed from whole to part".

A child's capacity to perceive in parts or to have various qualities of an object through sense organs is limited. He appreciates the wholeness of an object easily rather than to understand its various components to assimilate and understand its reality. His mental capacity is not capable to analyse and then to form a complete picture of the phenomenon under study.

Previous Knowledge: Apperception

It is emphasized from the above discussion that to bring home the child with a novel fact, two conditions are essential, i.e., a total situation at the outset and also the use of 'appreciative mass'. This means that in the study of a topic or a subject, the students should be told in advance the problem of which they have to find a solution. The total situation also constitutes the classroom environment. The teacher must present apperception, which is a sort of insight of the problem in view. It is a past experience or previous knowledge which makes the problem or a subject comprehensible, and interesting.

Observation

The process of observation is richer than perception and gives a child wider experiences about phenomena. It includes seeing the object closely, analysing its usefulness and also associating it with the knowledge of other objects. Perception makes us aware of the meaning of an object. But observation includes the intense thinking process about a phenomenon. It actually facilitates involvement wholeheartedly for seeking closely and fully the meaning of the object in view.

A class teacher unfolds a chart and displays it to pupils or draws a diagram on the blackboard. He makes the whole class involved in the process of observation. The teacher asks questions about the diagram drawn, and thus invites the attention of the pupils to the chart or the diagram drawn on the blackboard. An intense thinking process and interaction take place among the pupils and the teacher.

J.H. Meumann has mentioned the categories of observation: Purposive, non-purposive and purposeful. Purposive observation seeks reasons behind the phenomenon and leads the observer to find out its various elements and conditions of occurrence.

Non-purposive observation is meaningless and the observer unexpectedly becomes attentive towards the phenomenon. For example, a reader is busy reading a book. Accidentally two cats appear before him, quarrelling. They attract the reader. He observes the cats without any meaning. The cats in a few minutes disappear out of his sight. The observer again becomes involved in the reading of the book. His observation about the cats has no meaning for him.

Purposeful observation is not concerned with the investigation of the reasons, anxiety and curiosity about the phenomenon. The observer keeps himself busy with the search for novel conditions about the insight related to the observed object or subject. The purpose of the observer is to work under new situations other than the already existing ones so that he may know the real purpose of the subject.

Education and Observation

There is little power of observation during infancy and it is the duty of a teacher to allow children between the age group of one and five years to observe objects like toys, dolls, movable articles and also the neighbourhood environment. They may be allowed to visit railway station, post office, gardens, museums, banks, market, fairs and exhibitions. This may develop in children the habit of seeing, identifying, examining and memorizing different types of places. But infants know their environment only through sensations, particularly those of vision, hearing, touch, taste and smell. The power of observation is succeeded generally by sense training. Infants experience the sensation of heat and cold, hunger and thirst, pain and pleasure.

Children during school education must be frequently provided to handle objects themselves. They are allowed to get a feel of the apparatus with their own hands. This practice develops in them the power of thinking, memorizing and analysing the various functions of objects. They will have the training of learning through methods like heuristic, self-activity, Dalton plan, etc. Let pupils develop habits of observing pictures, charts, models and diagrams based on text lessons. This must be incorporated in the teacher's pointed questions.

Attention and Interest

Attention and interest are very much interrelated. A young child is interested in toys, dolls, shining and movable objects, coloured articles. He or she takes a lot of interest in these objects and never wants to part with these.

A child takes interest in listening to stories and compels parents to tell stories. Individual attention is fixed only on such objects or events in which he is interested. Attention creates readiness in a child for concentration on a specific object for which he has inherent interest. Therefore, it is a universally accepted notion that due to interest, an individual pays attention to an object. Interest is necessary for attention. Psychologically speaking, interest is a motivating power which binds attention in the mental process of an individual. Let us discuss, therefore, the various aspects of attention from the point of view of the classroom teaching process.

Classroom Teaching and Attention

In a classroom, the teacher creates interest by drawing a diagram on the blackboard. The pupils begin to analyse and think about the figure drawn. Their attention deepens by and by, so long as the children get involved in its meaning and thinking about its characteristics. This is only because of the fact that pupils find some novel ideas in the diagram. A novel idea is generated by the diagram. Thus, pupils pay attention to the diagram to the degree to which they have found novelty in it. It is, therefore, advisable that the teacher must draw an adequate diagram for creating inherent interest or novel ideas related to the subject or topic under discussion.

Children pay attention to those statements of the teacher which fulfil the motive of the lesson they are studying. It is the motive behind the teacher's activities in the classroom which keeps children interested from the beginning to the end.

In the introduction of the lesson, there must be a novel device to be presented before the pupils to make them interested. These may include charts, models, demonstrating apparatus, magic lamp, overhead projector, coloured slides, statements of renowned personalities, pictures and even the personal experiences of the teacher. In order to develop the power of attention in children, the teacher should place before them the teaching materials in which they may be interested because of their mental age.

Herbert and Dewey: Novel Activities

According to Herbert Spencer, individuals take interest only in those phenomena of which they possess some previous knowledge. Therefore, the teacher should make an effort to train pupils in a multitude of subjects so that they may develop various types of interest. But John Dewey does not favour Herbert's notion. Dewey's concept holds that novel ideas are created not by new knowledge, but by novel activities. Therefore, to develop interest, children should be trained by providing them with opportunities for performing self-activities. Experiences are based on activities and not simply on ideas which might disappear shortly. Dewey's project method has become popular in education from beginning to the end.

To sum up the discussion, the teaching process should not be monotonous, and of the same tone and nature. It should be punctuated with various types of teaching materials: interaction, demonstration, drawing diagrams, displaying charts, using technical aids, experiments and using CDs, video-screening, films, etc. The motive should not go out of the teaching process and interest should be maintained.

Teaching Process and Pupils' Interest

There are several challenges before a teacher to attract pupils towards his teaching process. The most important is interest of pupils. The teacher always keeps in mind the interest of pupils because that is what makes a person pay attention. Objects or stimuli must be either novel or abnormal for pupils to get them attracted. A novel apparatus in the laboratory attracts pupils and they take care to learn its operation. An abnormally fat boy among a group of normal boys attracts immediate attention. Children easily get involved in playing with a movable toy or objects like train, dolls, etc. The teacher tries to demonstrate his ideas by movable items.

A diagram drawn on the blackboard attracts pupils to imitate the same in their notebooks. It also facilitates their power of thinking. The diagram must have some motive related to the lesson to make the students attracted, otherwise their interest is shifted shortly. Shifting of attention differs from person to person. Some are able to shift easily from one subject to the other, but others find it difficult.

Duration and repetition also play a role in catching attention. The matter to which the teacher wants his pupils to pay attention is repeated many times. Similarly, the longer the duration of the stimulus is, the less powerful becomes the resistance capacity. The longer duration of the same idea makes the pupils inattentive. Boredom sets in.

Overall, for the interest of pupils, their inherited powers, social environment, intensity of stimuli and purpose of teaching should be taken into consideration.

Social Learning and Classroom Teaching

Mental development of students is a matter of social behaviour in the classroom and school. Schools and educational institutions of higher learning are an important ground where people of various cultures and levels of society meet and share ideas. They interact with each other. This causes and brings desirable changes in their behaviour. It forms a channel of imitation and learning and develops certain positive habits in students. The participants acquire the traits by imitating others through elicitation and reinforcement. Thus, the classroom becomes the foundation of the desired behavioural changes. It is the basic space of the school where the pupils imitate the behaviour of the teacher because he reinforces the ideas again and again to mould the attitudes of pupils. Social learning is a continuous process and is generated by imitation. Non-participants in the classroom indirectly learn specific responses or behaviour patterns through observation. In a school, pupils are regularly reinforced through sitting attentively, writing clearly, completing their work and thereby picking up concepts in their proper form. The social learning in the classroom thus forms a source of training educationally and scientifically too.

Students learn by identifying the manner of working of their leaders or models. They earn praise, success, rewards and these are identified by others and have a great influence on the achievement of fellow classmates. The teacher who works with all sincerity and arduous labour to explain difficult concepts through new teaching devices influences pupils. They identify the teacher with respect and learn many things without it being known by the teacher. Thus, the classroom is the fundamental working place where learning may take place simply by observing the model class fellows and sincere teachers of repute. The teacher should remain conscious of the fact constantly that there are some weak students, who fail to copy the behaviour of intelligent students. The teacher should help them and ask model students to cooperate to bring the weak fellows in order.

There is a need of reinforcing students in the class by adequate reward or praise of their achievements or for positive responses immediately. It affects the behaviour of the pupils. They feel delighted and work move vigorously. To sum up, classroom is a social situation where pupils change their behaviour patterns through sympathy, imitation, suggestion, competition, and above all, by encouragement given by the teacher.

Conditions Affecting Social Behaviour of Students in the Classroom

Age and health are the primary conditions which affect social contacts and behavioural changes. With growth, children develop social relations and intimacy with their relatives and classmates. Social development cannot take place without perfect health. During infancy, a child who is weak physically does not show social intimacy as shown by others who keep a sound health. A diseased child gets extra attention and also love by family members. This causes mental disorder and the child becomes irritant and selfish. Such weak children develop an inferiority complex. In the classroom, the teacher must pay due care for their development and instruct their friends to encourage them during play and also during other classroom programmes like interaction, meetings and conferences, dramatics, vocabulary quiz, competitions such as recitation of poems, stories and puzzles, etc.

Activities like games and athletic programmes as well as amusement activities play a key role in the social development of pupils. They provide opportunities for social mixing up, cooperation and friendship. The mix-up is the source of change of habits and behaviour.

School campus is the field of social environment which gives space to the teachers' individuality, classmates' habits, character and friendship. Even the school library and laboratory, including students' common room, have their impact in reorganising pupils' behaviour and social intimacy. Society of students makes them learn and behave properly, to speak decently and to follow social norms, traditions and culture. The campus is the laboratory of keeping their members in a positive tone of social behaviour and keeps them away from the social vices, maladjustments and disorder. The process very much needs the close supervision of the school principal, discipline incharge and student leaders.

Role of Teacher in the Mental Development

A teacher should strive to achieve the goal of behavioural changes in pupils and to make their thinking positive, constructive and socially creative. The teacher can generate positive traits in the pupils through his teaching process, and by citing experiences of life. Textbook analysis is not enough. Pupils learn many qualities from the teacher's individuality and his systematic way of dealing with situations and by adaptability, sympathy and also by setting good examples and ideals.

The teacher in his classroom process must not forget to make use of his gregarious instinct. He should invoke pupils to take part in discussion and mock sessions of student union. He also tries to develop ideals such as truth, beauty and good. The teacher prepares active pupils who can take part in scouting, NCC, hiking, travels and tours, competitive activities, etc. These activities develop in pupils the spirit of cooperation, sincerity, leadership, and justice. It is also a source of development of ideals like patriotism, social service, and getting a sense of poverty and exploitation. Personality is developed through participation in extra-curricular activities.

Role of the teacher in the classroom is unique. He develops in his pupils the habit of collection of things full of natural beauty and of social importance like stamps, photographs, rare coins, books of renowned leaders, personalities and writers. The teacher arouses curiosity about things of national heritage. He can make his teaching process interesting by introducing puzzles and problems to solve. The teacher is the main figure who creates love and affection through the activities on the school campus and in the classroom.

QUESTIONS

Short Answer Type Questions

1. *Define:*
   (a) Innate Powers
   (b) Cognitive Behaviour
   (c) Piaget's Mental Development
   (d) Sensation
   (e) Perception
2. What is Gestalt view of perception?
3. What is 'process of observation'?
4. Role of attention in the classroom teaching?
5. What is social learning?

Average Answer Type Questions

1. Discuss conditions affecting social behaviour of pupils.

2. How is social learning effective in classroom teaching?
3. Briefly point out a teacher's role in the mental development of pupils.
4. What is the role played by family members in the development of a child's behaviour for social good?
5. Discuss cognitive behaviour due to school environment of pupils.
6. Discuss Piaget's cognitive development.

Essay Type Questions

1. Classroom Application of Piaget's Ideas
2. Mental Development and Education
3. Mental Faculties and their Development

References

Lindgren, H.C., *Educational Psychology in the Classroom*, Wiley, NY, 1956.

Mathur, S.S., *Educational Psychology*, Vinod Pustak Mandir, Agra, 1998.

Piaget, Jean, *Psychology of Intelligence*, Harcourt, NY, 1930.

Pressey, S.L. and F.P. Robinson, *Psychology and the New Education*, Harper, NY, 1944.

Skinner, C.E. et al., *Educational Psychology*, Prentice-Hall, NY, 1951.

Spearman, C., *The Nature of Intelligence and the Principles of Cognition*, Macmillan, London, 1923.

Thurstone, L.L., *Primary Mental Abilities*, University of Chicago Press, Chicago, 1938.

Verma, I.B., *Fundamentals of Educational Psychology*, Sri Ram Mehra, Agra, 1956.

Sharma, Yogendra K., *Textbook of Educational Psychology*, Kanishka, New Delhi, 2004.

8

Individual Growth

An individual's growth, of course, is a part of social growth, but it is much concerned with the qualities and traits of an individual, his capacities, moral attitudes, tastes, likes and dislikes. All individuals have a different character and they complete their tasks differently because of their varied developmental structure. Individual structure – within and outside – has a different set-up. It includes his maturity by age, intellect, experience and his training to attain a certain specific mental qualities. This also forms a part of an individual's aesthetic development, consisting of his power of creativity and appreciation for the tasks of his liking. All individuals have different aesthetic values which are evolved from his environment. The development of an individual, thus, is a result of various factors comprising personal abilities and traits.

Cognitive Development

Cognitive or mental growth is a major part of an individual's personality. It is the level of intelligence which has the potentiality to handle tasks. Its components are very many. But some of the major ones include the individual's memory, imagination, perceptions, language, concepts and the capacity to solve difficulties to complete the task successfully. Psychologists have constructed numerous tests to measure one's intelligence, i.e., abilities and capacities to handle the given task successfully.

In the classroom, the teacher provides various tests from time to time to keep children awakened about their attainment of a skill, which is the instrument of completing the work assigned to them successfully. Teacher's main role in the class is to guide children in a way that they may understand the problem and complete the task successfully. The teacher also creates in the classroom an environment which initiates children to catch and react to the problem successfully. The classroom environment may be created through charts, and figures, diagrams drawn on the blackboard or model and even by citing parallel examples.

Cognitive development is also innate and children acquire much from heredity. Beside this, the role of the family is very important. It is very aptly said that 'home is the best school of a child'. Child's education actually begins at home and parents, especially the mother, play a key role in firming up the child mentally to face problems. The upkeep of rooms of family members, including the child's own, also have an effect on the child's mental growth. Modern equipment at home help much to foster the child's intellect and inquisitiveness.

Mental development is also the product of the family's neighbourhood and school structure. A child develops gradually his contact with the surroundings. The circle of child's relationship apart from his family becomes wider and wider. His team of friends and schoolmates affects very much the child's mental capacities, traits and mental aptitude. It is the function of parents or guardians, and also of the school teacher, to keep a regular watch and see that the children may not pick up wrong habits and get involved in quarrels, jealously, hatred and ill-spoken words. The teacher must take care of his teaching methodology, curriculum, co-curricular activities and discipline in the classroom and on the playground to make the children's behaviour positive and productive. School activities must be so organized as to facilitate positive ideas, and ideals, objectives and values. Various functions, including festival ceremonies, national events and the ceremonies of freedom fighters, leaders, etc., should be organized and students should be trained and encouraged to participate. These all form a major part in the mental growth of children during their school period. These foster in children stability of thought, maturity to handle situations, and to work with cooperation. The child learns to follow the norms of morality and gradually opens up and helps others.

Role of Education in Development

Education is not just about class books and examination. It is a training for life and to make children ready to shoulder the responsibilities that come as they grow up and also to fulfil duties as a responsible citizen.

Education should focus on inculcating the following important psychological traits:

(i) an attitude of telling the truth, honesty, obedience, discipline

(ii) positive use of gregarious instinct through team work and through participation in co-curricular activities

(iii) practising qualities like cooperation, humanity, leadership, patriotism, social service, etc.

(iv) to increase knowledge through extensive tours, which make students open up

(v) developing habits of collecting such things which might promote cultural heritage and tradition

The teacher may promote in students a good moral character by praising and justifying good habits and condemning all bad things. He should punctuate his process of teaching in the class by quoting examples of noble leaders and nation-builders. Education should be a joy for children. This can be done by introducing puzzles and problems of daily life and also by creating opportunities allowing work and play simultaneously.

Overall Development

Individual development does not mean working towards a sound physique and motor development. It is also not simply the acquisition of cognitive skills like memory, imagination, attention and power of reasoning and judgement and understanding. It is the all-round development of children, which make them nobler citizens to shoulder the responsibilities of society and the country. An individual's all-round development is the product of his complete personality guided by a multitude of values, including sentiments having special significance for his or her character. Character means those special features of a personality that go into the making of a distinctive and purposeful individual.

Overall development of an individual is not a fixed state. It is a dynamic totality which sees constant change due to interaction with the environment. In the words of Munn, "Personality of an individual is his or her multi-facet or multilateral structure integrated by modes of behaviour, interest, attitudes, capacities, abilities and aptitudes. The integration of behaviour differs from person to person. The overall development rests in the individual when he or she is trained to face all sorts of odds and comes out of the complex web of a zig-zag life, and finally makes a unique adjustment to environment. It is the development evolved by organization within the individual through psycho-physical systems. It is not simply the collection of traits but it is the organization of the internal and external activities. It includes the external appearance, qualities, aptitudes and capacities, etc. It is actually the total quality of the individual's behaviour."

Teacher's Role in Personality Adjustment

A teacher's role in the classroom is to make efforts to see that all children can adjust themselves somehow in the process of teaching. It depends upon their varying personality traits. The teacher's main objective is to seek a balance between the requirements of students and the situations put forth through the process of teaching to develop overall qualities in the students. He, therefore, tries to take care that students may develop social values like love, recognition, respect, authority and self-consciousness, etc. These may prove beneficial to face the problem of adjustment in a group of classmates.

A teacher tries his best to remove obstructions which appear in the realization of adjustment. He or she remains on the feet to remove frustration among students.

Children in school generally face conflicting situations. It is actually a struggle between a person and his environment. Children have to face many difficulties in the classroom, and they suffer in the absence of any proper guidance. For example, sex conflict is very common. Our society considers sex as a problem and a secret event, and during adolescence sexual desires become stronger.

Boys and girls, in the co-educational institutions, remain eager to know more about each other. If it is not handled by the teacher skillfully, there may be many mishappenings which finally adversely affect the students' life.

Family conflict is also a common phenomenon in our country. Some children become delinquents because of the unfriendly or harsh environment at home and disorderly families. Following are some of the causes pertaining to disorderly family structure:

1. Quarrels among parents over treatment of young ones.
2. The behaviour of stepmother or father towards the offspring and children from the first mother.
3. Lack of parental affection for their children.
4. Poor economic conditions in the family, and unfulfilment of the basic needs of children.
5. Over-expectation by the parents for undue achievements of their children.
6. Always pointing out the deficiencies of their children in front of the neighbourhood.
7. Loose and undesirable or harsh discipline imposed.
8. Loose character of parents and unbecoming sexual relations.

It is essential for overall development of a person that he or she should be treated with love and affection by family members. Home conditions to a great extent determine the development of children. Therefore, a peaceful environment is essential in the family and there should not be a continuous rows or disagreements and quarrels among the parents. Besides these, there is an important role of schools to develop in their students: befitting moral character. Schools must have sound programmes for social and emotional development to fulfil the needs as required by the society and nation.

Humanism and Overall Development

The overall or total development of an individual's personality is not the product of the external appearance, qualities, aptitude and capacities, etc. It is the result of the interaction of the individual with the environment. A person makes all efforts to adjust himself somehow with his environment. This depends upon a generally accepted philosophy of humanism, which has influenced almost every field of knowledge. It aims almost to evolve a human being. It is the philosophy based on secularism, nationalism and it is also scientific. It seeks the realization of humanist values in the individual, who is an integral part of society. According to it, the aim of education is not the growth of intellect only; but it aims at complete development of the human personality. It enables man to solve individual and social problems. Humanism supports the democratic philosophy of education because it is based on democratic values of liberty, equality and fraternity. It seeks realization of peace upon the earth. Its approach is positive since it is based on team spirit and cooperation. It favours community programmes and community living. It aims to develop a society conducive to all-round human progress.

Humanism integrates various ideals which sponsor human welfare, public service and social work in education. It is thus an important instrument to apply human nature and promotes all-round development in individuals. Humanism is the basis for child-centred education. It is the amalgamation of knowledge, social control, social development and social heritage. Its aim is to make education open for all, to allow development of poor and rich alike. It works on a man's intellect as well as making him self-dependent, which enhance overall qualities of human beings.

Humanism and Education

The application of humanism in education can make classroom teaching being based upon human psychology. Before making children well versed in learning, the teacher must make efforts to know them. The teacher should orient co-curricular activities so that students may develop qualities in various fields of life. The development of social values is emphasized through the project method. Pupils become proficient in organization of school activities in the supervision of the management, the teachers and the peer students together. Humanism seeks to make learning liberal and democratic and to encourage responsibility, liberty, equality and fraternity.

Humanism education is secular and it aims at the realization of humanist values. According to humanism, education aims at complete development of the human personality. The sole purpose of humanistic education is to increase efficiency and happiness of human beings. It develops in pupils team spirit and cooperation. Community programmes make community living easy.

Humanism in education integrates psychological, sociological and eclectic tendencies in education. It supports child-centred education. It promotes knowledge, social control, social development and preservation of social heritage.

Humanism in education favours a liberal and flexible curriculum. Its scope is wide enough to include moral, religious and spiritual subjects. It favours the method of teaching based on human psychology. Theoretical ideas of humanism are integrated into co-curricular activities. They foster social virtues. Humanists believe in the philosophy of unity in diversity. Therefore, our national culture is the product of regional art and architecture. Besides this, it encourages the pupils from different parts of the country and other countries to contribute in our institutions to develop an international humanist cultural atmosphere. Shantiniketan of Tagore is an example.

QUESTIONS

Short Answer Type Questions

1. *Define:*

   (a) (1) Cognitive Growth (2) Classroom Environment (3) Gregariousness (4) Aptitude (5) Overall Development

   (b) What do you mean by overall development?

   (c) What is the role of education in the development of an individual?

   (d) Teacher's role in personality adjustment?

   (e) Philosophy of humanism?

Average Answer Type Questions

1. Discuss mental growth of an individual.
2. Explain the relation between classroom task and classroom environment.
3. How does a disorderly family structure affect a pupil's growth?

Essay Type Questions

1. Cognitive Development
2. Humanism and Children
3. Individual Development and Education
4. Overall Development of Individual

References

Allport, G.W., *Psychological Interpretation*, Henry Holt, NY, 1927.

Cattell, R.B., *Personality: A Systematic, Theoretical and Factual Study*, McGraw-Hill, NY, 1950.

Hartshorne, H., *Character in Human Relations*, Charles Scribner's Sons, NY, 1932.

Meyers, G.C., *Developing Personality in the Child at School*, Commonwealth Fund, NY, 1937.

Mowrer, O.W., *Learning Theory and Personality Dynamics*, Ronald, NY, 1950.

Wickman, E.K., *Children's Behaviour and Teachers' Attitudes*, Commonwealth Fund, NY, 1928.

Woodworth, R.S. and D.G. Marquis, *Psychology*, Methuen, London, 1949.

Part III

Learning, Motives and Individual Differences

9

Emotions and Sentiments

Application in the Classroom

When someone is angry or in fear or in love, his mood, expression and facial impressions are quite different from his normal behaviour. Human behaviour and achievements are affected by such things as the state of fear, anger, joy, love, etc. These also affect social relations of individuals. These feelings of children are of great value for parents, family members, teachers and friends of their age. These feelings are mental conditions and known by psychologists as emotions. Emotional development is related with behaviour attitude, and therefore it is significant for education. It has a great bearing on the education of children, infants, young ones and even adults. According to A.T. Jersild, 'emotion' is a state of being moved, stirred up or aroused in some way. It involves feelings, impulses, physiological reactions, etc.

Importance

In his state of emotions, an individual can perform many amazing activities. He unexpectedly overcomes difficult situations. In the classroom, a teacher can make pupils learn difficult problems, and can make them understand difficult concepts by exciting their emotions. In building the character of students, their emotions have to be controlled and directed towards positive behaviour by providing adequate responses by the teacher. Due respect can be paid to them during the state of self-assertion, and they should be given proper hearing for their ideas, experiences and critical situations. They should be given proper lessons to subside anger by sympathy, pity, wonder and equanimity.

It is very important for the teacher to plan lessons in a way which may assist in pupils adjustment with complex situations. Emotions can be moulded and transformed for better adjustment and the emotional development in pupils, therefore, is studied in relation to their economic, cultural and social situations.

Causes Arousing Emotions

There are many situations in the classroom which arouse emotions. It is essential for a teacher to make a proper study and evaluation of pupils' behaviour – their needs, interests and goals. The teaching material and contents, instructions and guidance are so organized as to arouse in pupils the eagerness to learn without unwanted hurdles. It is possible when the pupils are made aware that the process is taking them towards the realization of their objectives stated in the beginning of the lesson. The laboratory in the classroom has many objects and things required to be handle scientifically. Their demonstration by the teacher may arise curiosity, wonder and novel experiences. This act by the teacher invigorates in pupils a change of behaviour in attitude. They too imitate in the same manner to complete the assignment.

The cause of emotion or feeling is very much related to one's pleasantness or unpleasantness. The very first step for a teacher to take should be to arouse a feeling of joy or pleasure in the minds of pupils by introducing his lesson. This can be done by exhibiting some model, chart, diagram on the blackboard or by reciting a couplet or poem or by telling a story or by relating his own experience. Nowadays, with the introduction of several technical aids for teaching like audio-visual sets, CDs, etc., the teacher can use these and engage students so they begin to take interest in learning.

Stages

Emotions during the infancy, childhood and adolescence are different as described below:

Emotions and Stage of Infancy

This is the earliest stage and covers the first six years of life. During this period, a child feels distress and delight, affection and anger, and also fear. These emotions in a child are more or less natural and he is unable to control their expression. If someone acts according to his desire and no one forbids him to act in his own way, he feels delighted. Contrary to his desire, if someone checks him or disturbs him, he feels angry, weeps, cries and even strikes. He shows an emotion of joy when his mother takes him in her lap. But if any member of the family gives his toys to someone else, he expresses anger. A child at the age of 4–6 years is possessive and shows ownership. He also begins to show signs of making or remodelling his articles at his own will. His expression during infancy varies a lot and for experiencing emotions he needs adequate stimuli. In the state of loneliness and darkness, coupled with unusual sounds, he expresses extreme fear. Excessiveness of an emotional state is harmful during this period.

The teacher allows children during the period of infancy to indulge in self-activity, playing and taking care of various kinds of toys. He learns on his own. But care should be taken to check the child from picking up quarrels, jealousy and to hit others of his own age.

Emotions and Stage of Childhood

Childhood is mostly spent being busy in school activities and among the company of friends in and outside the locality. Learner feels happy and expresses joy over his achievements and always tries to seek new channels for completing his tasks. If he is unable to get opportunities to progress, he remains annoyed and sometimes expresses irritation. There are many programmes in the school, and if he does not get a chance to participate, he expresses his anger. The role of the teacher is to sympathize and also to help the child in those programmes which are within his capacity and skill. The relations between young pupils and teachers should not have the fear complex. The teacher must not express publicly about the failure of any pupil. His weakness should be removed by motivating him through the activities in which he can do better. It is the prime function of a teacher to make the pupil aware of the objectives for which he or she attends the class, and to make him constantly aware of the potentialities he possesses. At the same time, the teacher lets his pupils know about realities, and to prepare them regularly to adjust with his thoughts and feelings. The child must be taught to face the ups and downs, and also to have amicable relations with classmates.

During the stage of childhood, the teacher faces two problems with pupils: anger and fear. These can be handled by providing constructive assignments. The teacher should try to understand the motive or purpose behind the angry behaviour of the pupil and this can be subsided by asking him to speak about the task he has done with success. The teacher must praise the pupil for his good work. This may avoid the provocation which he may have developed on account of the bad performance in any other assignment. As far as possible, he should not be disguised or ridiculed.

Fear can be avoided by introducing new situations. Fear of examination is common among pupils. The result is that the child suffers from the fear of failure. The teacher should tell them through examples of hard work by pupils that they can fare better in the examination without fear.

Pupils should be encouraged to face examination with confidence and with their abilities and capabilities. Presence of good ideals in the school's healthy environment may develop confidence among pupils to face the fear complex squarely.

Stage of Adolescence

Adolescence is a period of intensive changes in behaviour between 12 and 24 years of age. It involves changes in physical, mental and emotional aspects and affects the individual's personality entirely. Some of the individuals despite their advanced age behave like children and they act like children and become overjoyed and are two sensitive to act normally even in the ordinary situations. They lack in facing the problems sanefully. Emotional students in their classroom are not able to grasp the learning process in the correct perspective, and express their ideas without understanding underlying meanings.

Adults display extreme emotions in the form of anger, fear, hatred, pleasure, etc. But some of the pupils in the classroom have a balanced emotional behaviour. They act with their classmates calmly and try to mix with them because their ideas are generally based on common social values.

Teacher's Role in Dealing with Emotional Behaviour

In the classroom, it is not an easy task to understand pupils' emotional behaviour. The teacher's role is to control children through sublimation of their emotions. He tries to instil in them the notion of right conduct and good habits. They need occasional praise for curiosity expressed for novel ideas. Sublimation of emotions does not mean suppression or repression. It actually moulds pupils' feelings and checks the pitfalls of emotional complexes.

Emotionally infested adults need social status. The teenagers in the classroom are eager to get their approval by classmates. Therefore, the teacher should try to foster an environment in the class so that emotional sufferers are accepted by other students. It is essential to develop in them self-confidence and a sense of security. The teacher should provide all possible opportunities to them so that they could reflect confidence in games, seminars, debates, recitation and other co-curricular activities. Their emotions can be remoulded by assigning them a position of status in the class, and also affording the monitor's job and leadership roles in various activities of the school.

Adults who are neglected at home and school suffer from insecurity and generally remain misfit. Therefore, they need love and affection by the members of society. The teacher should see to it that emotionally suffering students are not allowed to fall in situations which pose a threat to their status and approval. Emotionally weak pupils develop unwanted fear of failure in examinations or losing good grades. They also remain in an awkward position because they develop a fear of their teachers. They, thus, become hostile, aggressive and pessimistic in their behaviour. Many a times they bunk classes, and may also revolt against teachers. It is very essential, therefore, that emotional students should not be left alone and neglected. The teacher should guide them and give them a place in various projects in the classroom. For emotional sublimation, they need close attention, love and sympathy of teachers. All possible opportunities should be provided to them so that they feel independent and shoulder responsibilities. They should be freely allowed to learn new things and to participate in adventure activities. This would prove to be a strong driving force in their future course of action in life. Most of the students who have already ushered in their adulthood remain eager for participating in adventure and thrilling activities. The teacher should give them opportunities and allow them to do new things and to visit new places so that they may gain experiences. It is the key for making them proficient in solving emotional problems.

Emotions of students are reflected in all their activities at school. Therefore, school programmes should be so organized as to suit the learners, and students must feel joy in their performances. Contrary to this, if the programmes arouse displeasure and fear, these may threaten the learners with failure or threaten to expose their weakness.

Besides this, relations between the learners and teachers reflect each other's emotions. These should be harmonious, even and uniform and without any favouritism, otherwise these may cultivate a deep dislike. Favouritism may develop hatred and some of the sufferers may revolt against their teacher. Therefore, the job of a good teacher in the classroom must be sensitive enough to emotions and must promote evenly friendliness and affection to all without any prejudice or favour. The concept of seasoned emotion should also be applied in case of teaching any subject or skill. The teacher's main objective is to help each learner so that each may develop to his or her potential. The teacher should see to it that each of the learners face reality and live with comfort with feelings of friendliness with others. In the classroom, it is essential that each learner be helped to understand his or her emotions and also those of others through experiences. It depends totally on such influences as are developed by the teacher's behaviour and also the atmosphere within the school and classroom.

Emotion and Sentiment

Emotion is a temporary phase and feeling and it disturbs the individual for a short time. But sentiment is a permanent emotion and lasts even when emotion has passed. Emotion is a mode of experience, and a way of activity. But sentiment is a fact and is related to an internal structure of an individual. When many emotions regarding an individual are formed and confirm the original emotion, they become part of the internal structure, to be known as sentiment.

Individuals display sentiments as guided by their traditional and culture. In this regard, William McDougall opines that sentiments are an essential part of an individual's character. Each individual has a different set of sentiments and the set is an effective organization of the individual process of learning. In other words, sentiments are social values which provide significant pattern to the character of an individual. Character of a learner is nothing but a system of sentiments. It is much more than a temporary phase as of an emotion. Each individual possesses a different type of character because each possesses a unique set of sentiments. The set of sentiments is based on the particular type of social and cultural environments of each individual. It is, therefore, a learner's life in the home, school and among fellows or classmates and neighbourhood. But this fact should not be overlooked that sentiments are formed with the organization of emotions. Emotions – acquired as well as innate – contribute in the formation of sentiments, which when equipped with the learner's mental and psychological traits and social and cultural dealings become part of character. Therefore, the character of a learner is not an internal or innate tendency. It is the product of the learner's evolution in the sets of his social and worldly environment.

The teacher's role in the classroom is to develop high sentiments in his students. It depends much on the learners' effective psychological traits and behaviour. Learners adapt from their teacher many habits and they try to emulate things like his speech and actions. The conduct of the teacher, therefore, should be sympathetic, full of love and affection, helpful and tolerant towards all pupils without prejudice and selfish to some. McDougall has stressed repeatedly that a sentiment of self-regard is to be developed for character building. It comprises the values of love, friendship and self-help. Love is more effective than punishment and hatred. 'Spare the rod and spoil the child' has been psychologically disregarded as the maxim of education. Louis Munford has assigned punishment as a totally negative function. It cannot be effective in helping the development of positive character in the learner. John Henrick Pestalozzi too was not in favour of punishment, and stressed that its use should be avoided as far as possible. Punishment causes a loss of confidence and creates hatred.

QUESTIONS

1. How can fear be overcome?
2. Give examples and suggest ways to avoid anger.
3. Discuss emotional development during childhood.
4. Discuss relationship between emotion and sentiment.
5. What are various methods used generally in the classroom by teacher to deal with and channelize emotions?
6. Give various characteristics of emotional maturity and illustrate your answer with suitable examples.

References

Chaubey, S.P., *Child Development*, L.N. Agarwal & Sons, Agra, 1986.

Crow, Lester D. and A. Crow, *Educational Psychology*, Eurasia, New Delhi, 1964.

Freud, S., *The Problem of Anxiety*, Norton, NY, 1936.

Gates, G.S., 'An Observational Study of Anger', *Journal of Experimental Psychology*, Vol. 19, Issue 4, 1929.

Hadfield, J.A., *Mental Health and Psychoneurosis*, George Allen, London, 1952.

Hawkes, G.R. and D. Pease, *Behaviour and Development from 5 to 12*, Harper, NY, 1968.

Hurlock, E.B., *Adolescent Development*, McGraw-Hill, NY, 1949.

Jersild, A.T. and F.B. Holmes, *Children's Fear*, Columbia University, NY, 1935.

Jersild, A.T., *Educational Psychology*, Macmillan, NY, 1985.

Lindgren, H.C., *Educational Psychology in the Classroom*, John Wiley, NY, 1956.

May, R., *The Meaning of Anxiety*, Ronald, NY, 1950.

10

Learning and Motivation

Application in the Classroom

An individual learns when he begins to act to satisfy his urge. It is only an urge or motive which compels a human being to behave in a particular way. Our behaviour is the product of our needs. We search water when we are thirsty. If we have no thirst, we neglect a well of water, tank or pipe. It is an urge or our thirst which compels us to drink. This urge is nothing but a motive.

Motives are need-based. Needs differ from individual to individual and methods of meeting them also differ because of different levels of learning of individuals. Every individual has some natural dispositions which are motives, according to American psychologists. But some psychologists call motives as instincts which compel an individual to act in a particular direction to meet a particular problem.

R.S. McDougall describes instinct as our innate disposition which compels us to perceive the given situation, to experience emotional excitement and to act in regard to it in a particular manner. The following are the instincts and related emotions:

Instinct	*Emotion*
Escape	Fear
Repulsion	Disgust
Curiosity	Wonder
Pugnacity	Anger
Self-assertion	Positive Self-feeling
Self-abasement	Subjection
Parental	Tender emotion
Gregariousness	Loneliness
Acquisitiveness	Ownership
Constructiveness	Creativity
Food Seeking	Appetite
Sex	Lust
Appeal	Distress
Laughter	Amusement

It is clear that instincts are affected by intelligence. Different motives compel an individual towards a particular work. Motives are need-based and our conduct is controlled by our needs. Motives are innate and acquired by their nature. Innate motives are natural needs such as hunger, thirst, sleep, sex, etc. Acquired needs are those which are born during our life as a result of the effect of our surrounding environment. An individual also acquires needs due to his education and also through the manner in which he is brought up. Motives are also social and personal. Individuals are different because they move in different structure of societies. Their desires and experiences differ because of their different social culture. In a similar society, motives are generally common and individuals develop common experiences. These may be called public or social motives. For example, 'sufism' favours motives like simplicity, purity and tolerance without complexities in life. Individual interests and attitudes give rise to personal motives. Some individuals are materialistic in their needs while others are idealistic and their needs differ because of their different attitudes towards life. Interests are personal. But personal motives can be changed through time, experiences, age and by learning.

Needs and Motivation

Motives, as has been seen above, are our needs and these differ from motivation. Motivation is a process of learning which can mould, change or alter personal ideas and thoughts. It can create interest which was formerly absent in an individual. In the classroom, a teacher can invigorate new ideas and interest in pupils using adequate psychological methods and teaching techniques. Educationally, motivation is a sort of capsule which invigorates in pupils the ideas and capabilities to understood the given problem. The process of motivation involves the use of sophisticated materials and devices of learning techniques. Motivation moves pupils towards set objectives of learning. Therefore, H.W. Bernard has defined motivation as the process of learning which initiates in pupils those approaches that make them eager for the kind of learning the school endorses.

Motives and Motivation

Motives or needs differ from motivation. Whatsoever our needs are, they move us toward action. Motives are internal factors which move an individual to act and to sustain. In other words, psychologically speaking, motive includes only those factors which control the activity of the living being. But educationally, motive is a sort of practice satisfying a particular need, and is different from reflex action. But motivation is all above the practice of satisfying needs. It is a technique to stimulate learning in the pupil to grasp the problem. It is a psychological process and initiates the pupil internally to solve the problem or satisfy the need. It makes the fulfilment of the task in hand comprehensibly easy. It is the process which changes pupils' behaviour to understand the problem. For example, to add something in the classroom is motivation. It changes the classroom environment and it is so directed through technical changes that it fosters thinking of the pupils to achieve the desired goal.

Types of Motivation

There are generally two types of motivation which may keep pupils active in the classroom: (a) natural, and (b) artificial.

Natural motivation is related to the innate tendencies and impulses of the individual. Intention to learn is natural and it is present in some, while in others it may be of diffusing nature. It is very essential for a teacher to create in his students the intention to learn: pupils' nature must be ready to accept what the teacher aims to create through his process of teaching and through the expression of ideas. Young ones are interested in play and amusement. If the teacher coordinates his narration by using some instances and examples from games like cricket, hockey, football, etc., the pupils become alert and ready to listen to the lecture. The teacher's changed narration thus is motivation and the ideas involved therein stimulate the learners. This type of motivation is known as natural and this is the reason why Montessori and Kindergarten first use the playway system for creative education.

Pupils also feel at home when examples are given which invigorate them to imitate their heroes' actions. If a teacher punctuates his expression through couplets from tales of 'Jhansi ki Rani' or 'Haldighati', pupils become active to listen to the chivalrous deeds of their heroes. The faculty of their imagination is strengthened in respect of imitation and they are motivated for a particular activity. It is a natural tendency of youngsters and it sets them in motion to do so accordingly. Natural tendencies and feelings of love and respect for personalities of their liking create in them an extra force for learning and creation. They imitate and construct wonderful items beyond our imagination.

Natural motivation is also related to a healthy body and an alert mind. It is aptly said that it is mind and healthy body which allow as to act consciously and to receive positive ideas. Peaceful mind and healthy physique computably allow children to acquire knowledge, affection, cooperation, leadership, comforts, success, etc. These may be utilized by a teacher as natural motivation for learning.

Artificial motivation is a force mainly related to the school environment and classroom equipment. If a school has an adequate playground, library, a room for dance, drama and co-curricular activities like swimming pool, etc., naturally these become an incentive for motivation.

A teacher in the classroom must set his goal for a lesson he wants to deliver. Pupils are attracted to receive instructions with ease provided the goal itself is clear. Clearer the goal, the more forceful is the motivation concerned with learning. A good teacher always try to fix his pupils' attention towards the goal by using blackboard, charts, models and also by his expression and encourages them to act for successful achievement. He keeps his pupils' attention fixed towards the goal by interaction and also by encouragement. A teacher is careful to stimulate his pupils by following the curriculum prepared carefully according to pupils' age, ability, capacity, etc., to grasp and to promote the level of their understanding. The curriculum which is prepared properly enhances the possibilities of setting specific goals. It makes teaching strengthened because it is according to pupils' strength and limitations.

Pupils are also motivated by making them understand the progress of their learning periodically. Therefore, the teacher judges their progress by arranging periodical tests and lets the pupils know their strength and weakness. The periodical tests motivate pupils to work with care to achieve more. The tests create in them a positive attitude and inspire them to perform better. If students know their progress of work, they feel pleasure or pain, satisfaction or dissatisfaction. They work more vigorously to achieve greater satisfaction by following properly the required goal of learning.

Teachers must encourage pupils and reward them for their good work. Reward is a direct motivation. It makes the rewardee work with greater vigour and force. Reward is the source of creating ability for constructive work. It is also a source of developing a competitive spirit among pupils. As against punishment, reward is considered more fruitful. Reward can be given through praise and honour before the entire group of classmates. It is also given by awarding a 'certificate of honour'. But pupils are heartily motivated if they get reward in the form of materials like books, articles or useful things, etc.

Punishment is a negative motivation and is generally discarded by psychologists. Punishment develops a fear tendency and discourages the wrong doers. Punishment is a sort of deadlock for work and pupils try to avoid doing things for fear of being punished again. In schools, the practice of inflicting cruel and corporal punishment is no more in vogue. The fear of punishment is more harmful than motivation for further improvement. It causes frustration and an inferiority complex. The punished child generally boycotts work. It generally checks initiative and adversely affects the character of pupils. Their personality too is distorted.

Motivation and Learning

Motivation and learning are interrelated. There can be no learning without using adequate methods. Adequacy is a sort of motivation for learning. The learning process cannot take place without motivation. For example, thirst and hunger are motives and these create a drive in an individual to act. Pupils act vigorously for earning wealth, honour, etc. The experiment of E.L. Thorndike shows that a hungry creature by providing food learns something successfully. This shows an intimate relationship between learning and motivation.

Classroom Activities and Motivation

A teacher in the classroom makes the goal of his lesson quite clear and applicable to life experiences by using adequate means of motivation. He should introduce new techniques to motivate. This does not mean that he neglects traditional means like the use of blackboard. Thus, there is a close relation between old methods and newer techniques to provide adequate means for motivation. Motivation should be always directed towards the fulfilment of major objectives of the teaching lessons.

Motivation may be in the form of some activities such as conducting experiments. It should invariably by reinforced with the participation of learners. The pupils should be given proper opportunities to participate in experiments. It is the source of inspiration for learning. The experiment should be so initiated that the pupils feel self-motivated. Students possess their own prestige, and they are encouraged through group work. The teacher should utilize their spirit of cooperation.

A teacher's main objective is to develop positive behaviour in pupils. Positive behaviour is the product of achievement of the desired objectives. These may be successfully achieved through the means of adequate motivation given to pupils as per their needs during the process of teaching. Needs of students and also the objectives of the teaching process are required to be coordinated by

Figure 10.1

Diagrammatic Representation of Seriated Process of Motivation

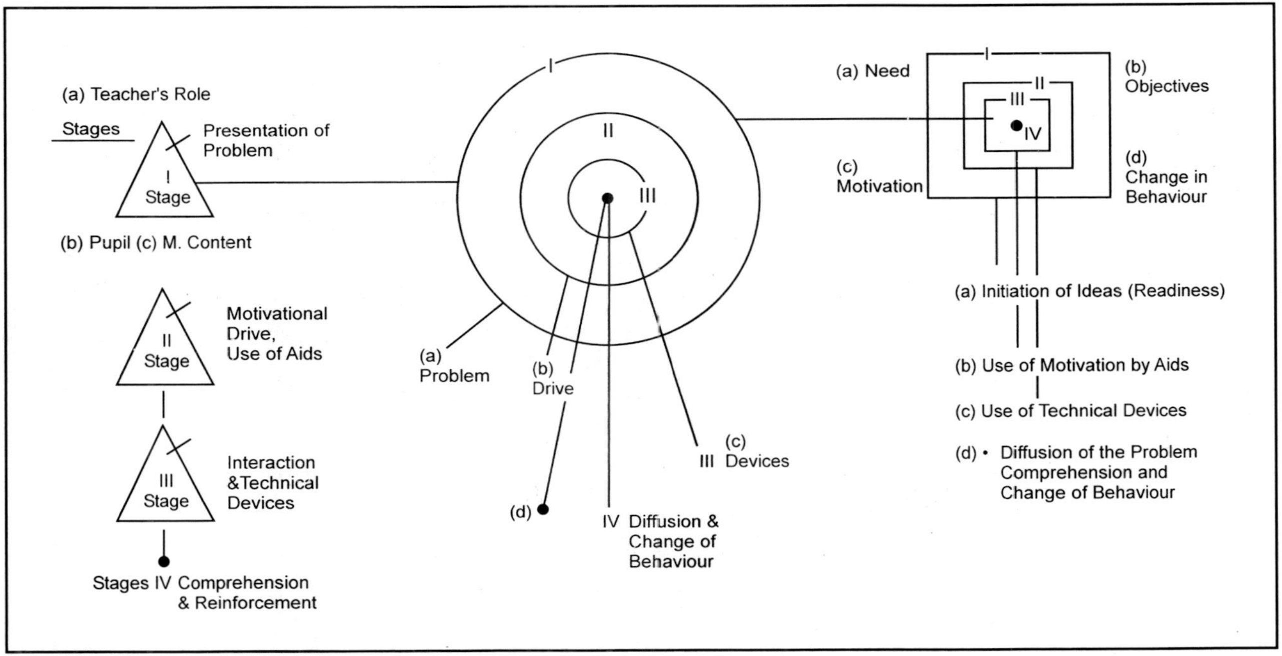

motivation. A successful teaching process depends a lot on the effective motivation provided to solve the difficult aspects of the learning. Figure 10.1 explains the seriated process of learning through the role of teacher to diffuse the problem and remove inhibitions in the way of the desired behavioural changes in the pupils by motivation.

The figure represents the seriated process of motivation. It is a three-dimensional effort involving the role of the teacher to use motivation with the intention to promote learning.

The I Stage represents presentation of the problem before the group of pupils according to their needs, objectives or goals with a view of changing their ideas and behaviour through the given content. It initiates their thinking and creates in them the readiness to interact.

The II Stage represents beginning of the activity according to needs or drive of children. The use of certain aids as motivation drives learners and make them feel about the goals. He tries to analyse his thinking and a little change takes place in his mind. The use of aids is an additional stimuli to learning.

The III Stage promotes interaction between the teacher and the taught because of the knowledge gained through technical devices and their exhibition by the teacher. It is the stage when the learner's attitude is changed and he becomes capable to grasp the problem.

The IV Stage is the final effort, which is actually the result of the motivational process. The learners comprehend the situation and their behavioural changes are reflected in their favourable reaction to the problem in hand. The problematic situation is comprehended and gradually solved.

QUESTIONS

Short Answer Type Questions

1. *Define:*

   (a) Motives, Instincts, Emotions, Drives, Artificial Motivation.

   (b) What is Pavlov's experiment?

   (c) Who used play as an instrument of learning in education?

   (d) What do you mean by a goal of learning?

Average Answer Type Questions

1. Discuss the difference between instinct and emotion by giving examples.
2. Discuss the role of need during motivation used by a teacher.
3. Discuss natural motivation.
4. How are learning activities and motivation related?

Essay Type Questions

1. Application of Motivation in the Classroom
2. Seriated Process of Learning
3. Internal and External Motivation

References

Allport, G.W., *Personality: A Psychological Interpretation*, Henry Holt, NY, 1937.

Bernard, H.W., *Psychology of Learning and Teaching*, McGraw-Hill, NY, 1972.

Bloom, B.S., *Taxonomy of Educational Objectives*, Longmans, NY, 1965.

Bugelski, B.R., *Learning and Motivation*, Henry Holt, NY, 1956.

Burton, W.H., *The Guidance of Learning Activities*, Appleton, NY, 1952.

Gagne, R.M., *The Conditions of Learning*, Holt, NY, 1970.

Guthrie, E.R., *The Psychology of Learning*, Harper, NY, 1935.

Hilgard, E.R., *Theories of Learning*, Appleton, NY, 1948.

Lindgren, H.C., *Educational Psychology in the Classroom*, John Wiley, NY, 1956.

Simpson, R.H., *Improving Teaching Learning Process*, Longmans, NY, 1953.

Stacey, C.L. and Others, *Understanding Human Motivation*, Howard Allen, Cleveland, 1958.

11

Learning and Educational Implications

Learning activity poses several basic questions. What to learn? Why to learn? Where to learn? Who makes us learn? It is not easy to answer these. Do we learn in a school or in our home or without any formal agency? Are we required to know the language, numbers to learn? Do we not learn many things without any aid or institution? What about self-learning? Who makes a newborn learn to suck milk? Who makes us learn to walk, run, laugh or weep? These questions need care and the sense to be answered in the right perspective.

It is a fact that as soon as we are born, learning begins to take place in the lap of our mother and in the arms of our father. Learning is an innate tendency and we learn to run, to play, etc., without any help. We are surrounded by many things. We see and adjust. We imitate nature and learn from environment. This is known as 'adaptation' to a natural situation. We gradually become young and grow. The growth makes us experience several tricks and traits of life. We enter from a simple environment of home and our mother, father and family and gradually face the complex environment of society. There we learn from experience and respond to the environmental situations. Thus, learning is a continuous process of life, enriched by the accumulation of experiences.

Our problem is: how to define the process of learning?

Concept and Definition of Learning

Learning means 'improvement' in our abilities for adaptation to our environment through experiences. We grow in age and learn gradually to adjust with our surroundings with the gained ability. This is known as maturation, enhancing our capacity of adjustment. R.S. Woodworth, therefore, defines learning as a process of development which adds newer experiences different from what it would otherwise have been. Learning is a sort of treatment for raw behaviour and it is a means to make an individual capable to solve hurdles in his life. Charles F. Skinner defines learning as an instrument which changes the behaviour through coordination of mind and the problem obstructing a smooth life. Our behaviour is changed many a times unconsciously with the change in our age or with the experiences we gain and learn through interaction with the novel environment. Therefore, J.P. Guilford defines learning as any change in behaviour resulting from behaviour which now is different from the one which we had before. It is simply a change because of our advancement in age. Our age and a change in our thinking which moulds our activities occur simultaneously and without our being conscious about the change. Learning, therefore, can be defined as a quality in behaviour which makes us organize our responses towards adaptability with situations by newly-gained habits. Learning actually is an organization of behaviour for better. Summing up the concept of learning, it may be defined as the process of change in behaviour through reacting to an encountered situation.

Factors of Learning

Thorndike in his treatise 'Educational Psychology' expresses those factors of learning which originate from certain laws. Three major laws give rise to several factors: (a) readiness, (b) exercise, and (c) effect.

We learn only when we are prepared to learn something. Our readiness for learning depends directly on our needs, objectives and a goal. It is necessary that we should make ourselves ready mentally to accept a change in our behaviour. In the classroom, therefore, a teacher tries to fix minds of pupils on specific objectives to achieve. The objectives are virtually needs which the pupils want to achieve through the instructions of and guidance of the teacher in a classroom.

The second law of exercise is concerned with the repeated application of a useful exercise. It consequently helps in the formation of habit, which is a necessity for change in our behaviour or learning process. But we like to repeat and fix our mind for repetition only when we understand the underlying meaning. In the classroom, the teacher compels pupils to understand the meaning of a poem and then insists on its repetition. Comprehension is a prior necessity for repetition.

The third law of effect is of utmost importance because it is the favourable effect which makes learning possible. Favourable effect means which is according to our needs. We learn in the classroom only those concepts which follow the stated objectives that our needs determine and make us ready to learn carefully. We learn Arithmetic, Science or Sociology only when these may prove helpful and effective in the future course of our life.

Besides the above three laws of Thorndike, the process of learning involves certain subsidiary factors like pupils' interest in the given work, interest for improvement of behaviour towards the traditional views, significance of newer ideas, our attitude towards the given problem and our keen attention for the fulfilment of motives.

Whatever has been discussed already, it is clear now that factors affecting learning include (a) age and maturity, (b) social environment, (c) kind of activity to be learnt, (d) learning by understanding, (e) learning in part or as a whole, (f) recitation, (g) active participation, and lastly, and (h) reinforcement by the teacher, i.e., praise or reward.

Methods of Learning

In the classroom, this is a problem for a teacher – how to teach or make pupils learn? Its a the question of creating an atmosphere in the class which may promote learning and which may help the pupils to learn with ease. This depends on methods employed by the teacher in the class. The following are psychological devices which may be used by the teacher in the class:

1. *Whole and part learning:* A teacher can ask pupils to learn the subject matter in its full sense. For example, a poem can be learnt in its full form at a time. But it is not an easy task and pupils find it difficult to memorize the entire poem at a time. They learn stanza by stanza easily.

   But speaking psychology, the poem can be easily learnt wholly provided its sense is taught before asking students to learn it by heart. The mind of learner picks up stanzas automatically provided the meaning of the each is well connected. Part learning takes much time and is not retained. Pupils are unable to understand its major theme and cannot appreciate its main objective. Thus, part learning is not capable of making a behavioural change and pupils lack in appreciating the major ideas of the given subject matter.
2. *Medium way between whole and part:* Many a time, the subject matter which is required to be learnt is very lengthy. It is a difficult task to learn it in one go. It is rather a waste of energy. It is better to remember the text paragraph by paragraph, carrying one full meaning of the phenomenon described. It is whole as well as part learning process. The learner does not feel tired and it avoids boredom psychologically. The subject matter may be divided into meaningful paragraphs to take up one by one. Later, the previously learnt parts should also be repeated along with the new paragraph to follow. Thus, parts taken together which are learnt along with parts to follow may be made to learn the whole easily and meaningfully.
3. *Recitation:* It makes learning easy. According to A.I. Gates, recitation is exercising as soon as possible. It results in economizing learning. The subject has to revise and recall the matter without looking at the written text several times. This method has advantages over other methods because it affects the economy of time and effort. It also has the merit of retention of what has been mastered.
4. *Spaced learning:* It is another method which facilitates learning. We can successfully learn two lectures per week over a period of six months, rather than 50-odd hours of instruction crowded into a week. The space interval is advantageous because it makes to settle the learning material in mind.

5. *Motivation and learning:* The best method of learning in the classroom which a teacher generally uses is a technique known as motivation. Motivation plays an important role in classroom teaching. If pupils are satisfied by the teaching process, they repeat it in their extra time, and, this facilitates learning. The teacher should encourage and reinforce pupils for their positive behaviour towards the subject matter. This sort of incentive helps learning and pupils feel elevated.

The teacher should be careful in reminding pupils during the process of learning about the goals or objectives to be achieved. Goal-bound practice facilitates learning. It also creates an interest in children and they enjoy themselves in repeating what they are being taught. The teaching material should be well planned so that it may invoke in pupils liking, along with changing their attitude and testing their level of intelligence. The motivation in the classroom must follow the curriculum, goal of learning, strategies of teaching, level of intelligence of the learners and their age.

Figure 11.1

Planning of Classroom Lesson

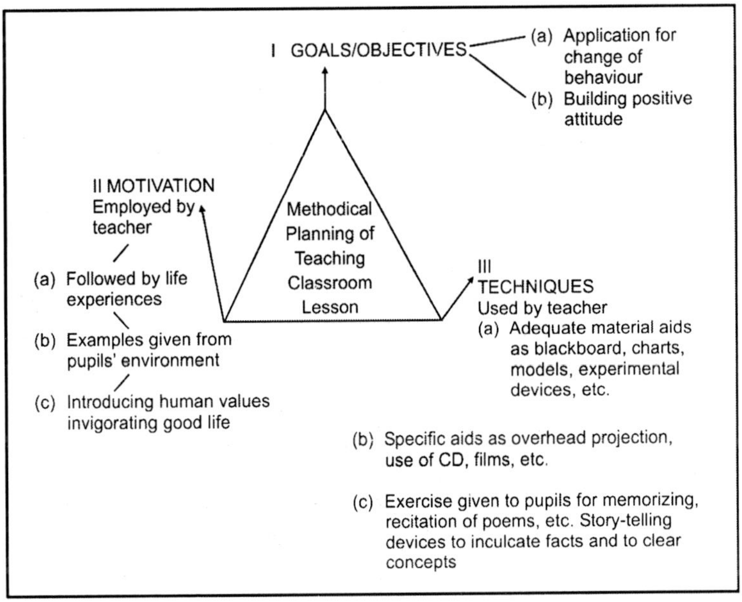

Figure 11.1 shows the major areas which have to be followed by a teacher in planning his daily teaching work.

Some devices to improve learning process are:

(a) *Intention or desire:* The teacher must see to it that there is the intention in the minds of pupils to learn. Without the desire for learning, it would be difficult to bring home to the children the ideas or concepts required to be learnt.

(b) *Learning matter should be enjoyable:* Pupils learn easily if the given matter is according to their interest. They grasp only if they feel pleasure and enjoyment. The teacher should incorporate examples from pleasant experiences. He should avoid indifferent material which is not pleasing and not according to the pupils' interest.

(c) The teacher by adequate rewards to successful pupils may invoke the spirit of competition among the group of pupils in the class. It is very necessary and psychologically appropriate to encourage pupils for performing better than last time.

(d) Devices involving filmstrips, models, CDs and other aids like charts, etc., and the use of overhead projector create interest for having novel experiences about distant areas and lands in foreign countries. The textbook matter about the western world or far-east countries may be presented by incorporating educational films of the corresponding areas. It makes learning effective, interesting and much near to the real situation which was formerly present in the form of imagination.

(e) The teacher should let the pupils know the result of the acquisition of their knowledge. The result may be declared by means of five-point scale such as ABCD, etc. The result of achievement known intermittently enhances the spirit of learning in pupils. The test papers with appropriate corrections should be shown to students for further improvement. The corrected test papers are a feedback for the learners.

Educational Implications of Learning

Formal education given in institutions must not be distant or detached from life experiences. Education guides our behaviour and instructs us to follow ideals which may be useful for our progress and development during our life journey. It depends on our aims for the fulfilment of our needs and comforts. The teacher plans his subject matter daily before it is delivered in the class. The plan should be based on the aims and objectives which we aim to develop.

The aims must be clearly expressed through introducing the lesson before the pupils in the class. The aims must be according to the needs and they must promote their attitudinal behaviour. To make the pupils ready to change their thinking for better adaptation to environmental situations.

The teacher should use the techniques which provide opportunities to children for interacting favourably with the environment through experiences they have had by means of instructions in the class.

Aims must be life-bound, and not for immediate problems. For immediate problems, the teacher may make clear their solutions by life experiences only as hints and let the pupils work out by their own efforts. The pupils may be provided working outlines to think about the problems and responsibility be given to each according to their ability. Competition for successful achievement and cooperation to handle the situation must continue together. The pupils need incentives for proper handling of the situation.

A school must not be understood as the only place where human beings receive education. But, it is a place where our young ones are disciplined for performing activities which are significant for our life-long journey. John Dewey defines school as a special environment where a certain quality of life activities are provided. This means that school conducts those activities which ensure development of child for a successful life journey. It is the place where pupils of different religions, castes and creeds and cultures get training for their harmonious development. School provides organized education where the provision for curricular and co-curricular and cultural activities is available. Pupils have opportunities for having education galvanized with equality, liberty and fraternity. It is the place where citizens of national ideals and responsibilities come out after getting training to face problems of various aspects.

QUESTIONS

Short Answer Type Questions

1. Define the role of a mother initiating the learning process during the period of infancy.

2. Discuss the role of nature in learning.
3. How do we learn from environment?
4. Discuss 'learning and adaptation'.
5. What do you mean by 'readiness' as a factor of learning?

Average Answer Type Questions

1. What is 'whole and part' learning?
2. Discuss Thorndike's law of learning and role of teacher.
3. Explain with examples the role of recitation in the teaching of literary lessons.
4. What are the major steps followed by a teacher to make learning comprehensible?
5. What are the essential elements followed by a teacher to make learning comfortable and easy?

Essay Type Questions

1. Learning and Classroom Environment
2. Learning Technology
3. Education and Learning

References

Bernard, H.W., *Psychology of Learning and Teaching*, McGraw-Hill, NY, 1972.

Bindra, D., *Motivation*, Ronald, NY, 1959.

Brown, F.J., 'Knowledge of Result as an Incentive in School Room Practice', *Journal of Educational Psychology*, Vol. 23, pp. 532–52.

Guthrie, E.R., *The Psychology of Learning*, Harper, NY, 1935.

Sears, P.S., *The Effect of Classroom Conditions on Strength of Achievement Motive and Work Output of Elementary School Children*, Stanford University Press, California, 1963.

Skinner, B.F., *The Technology of Teaching*, Appleton-Century, NY, 1968.

Traver, R.M.W., *Essentials of Learning*, Macmillan, NY, 1963.

12

Intelligence and Development of Pupils

Motivation is an important device which is used to promote learning in the classroom by the teacher. Motivation and learning together add much to raise the level of cognition and power of understanding of children. The upgraded mental development of pupils in the classroom increases their power of comprehension, intellect, mental capabilities, thinking, etc. The entire mental process, thus, is based on intelligence increased in pupils due to constant efforts of teachers by employing adequate devices for developing working or functional potentialities.

Intelligence has great educational implications. The contents of various syllabuses are generally graded stage-wise according to the level of pupils' intelligence. The teacher must understand the nature of intelligence which suits the attitudes of pupils. The teacher tries in the classroom through an incessant process of learning and also through the organization of the classroom environment to develop different mental powers or levels of intelligence.

What is Intelligence?

Intelligence is a sort of mental quality in an individual which makes him or her adjust comfortably in a new environment. Intelligence is a composite mental achievement which concentrates an individual's attention towards a specific motif, to imbibe in him the faculty of self-introspection and finally, makes him capable to face any problem in its correct perspective. According to L.M. Terman, intelligence comprises clear understanding for abstract objects, interrelationship between different things and the capacity for solving problems.

Intelligence is the mental power in an individual which makes him capable to think, reason and to understand the situation in its correct perspective. It is actually the learning ability gained by individuals from their experience, and it makes them adjust comfortably in a new environment, and above all, to grasp the situation correctly and solve the problem.

Definitions

According to H.G. Wells, In case of pupils, a teacher in the classroom seeks objectively to generate "properties which make students' behaviour positive so as to act better in a novel situation".

William Stern defines intelligence as an ability to adjust oneself in a new situation. Thorndike defines intelligence as the ability to make profitable use of past experience.

Truly speaking, intelligence is not simply a power of understanding to grasp the new situation. It is actually the conglomeration of multiple brain powers such as aggregation of an individual to act purposefully and to think rationally to deal effectively with his environment.

Summing up, intelligence is an organization comprising the abilities of readiness, correctness, and of understanding complicated and abstract things. Intelligence helps a person to control in necessity his mental power and action to solve problems.

The modern concept of intelligence is related with hierarchical abilities successfully learnt by incorporating those acquired earlier. It is the technique that a child acquires for processing information supplied by his senses through sound, sight, touch, smell and taste, etc.

Mental Age and Individual Differences

Physical age and mental age were a century back considered the same. Mostly pupils were either good or bad in terms of their intelligence. But now, children of mental age and chronological age are not considered the same. The behaviour of the two types – mentally and physically intelligent children – are also different.

Mental age, for example, means if a child of eight years could solve the questions meant for 10 years old children, the mental age of the eight-year-old child will be fixed at 10 years. Similarly, if an eight-year-old child succeeds in answering the questions meant for seven-year-old children only, he or she will be put in the mental age of seven years' category.

Mental age may increase or decrease because it is decided at the time of the intelligence test. Binet expresses mental ability of a child through two broad categories, i.e., higher or dull intelligence. If a 10-year-old child has the mental age of more than 10, then he is considered to he of higher intelligence. Contrarily, if the child of 10 years indicates the mental ability of only an eight-year-old child, he is then considered dull.

Intelligence Quotient (I.Q.)

L.M. Terman has devised a formula to express intelligence. It is known as 'Intelligence Quotient' or I.Q., and it is the ratio between chronological age and mental age, for example:

$$I.Q. = \frac{M.A.}{C.A.}$$

For avoiding fraction and expressing it in a whole number, the ratio is multiplied by 100.

i.e., $I.Q. = \frac{M.A.}{C.A.} \times 100$

For example, if a 10-year-old child attains 12-year mental age, his I.Q. will be 1.2 × 100 or 120.

Terman revised the relationship between a bright and a dull child by several experiments, and finally, he recommended a table showing I.Q. Varying among very superior child and other various categories down to the category of an idiot child.

Table 12.1

*Table of Terman Merrill**

I.Q.	*Categories*	*Classes (by % from Zero)*
140–169	Very superior	+ Genius
120–139	Superior	+ Talented
110–119	High average	+ Superior
90–109	Normal average	+ High Average
80–89	Low average	0 Average
70–79	Borderline defective	—
60–69	Moron	– Defective
50–59	Moron	– Moron
25–49	Imbecile	– Imbecile
0–24	Idiot	– Idiot

*Table of Terman Merrill: 'I.Q. on the revised Binet Scale', *Journal of Educational Psychology*, 1938, Vol. 29, pp. 641–651.

I.Q. and Causes of Individual Differences

Why are some pupils of the class more intelligent than others? Why are some below the average category in terms of I.Q.? Psychologists generally express two reasons for differences of the levels of I.Q. in case of individuals:

(a) Mostly it is found that children are like their parents or ancestors. In other words, the individual's intelligence is inherited. But there is no law which supports the inheritance of intelligence. Many cases are found by the teacher in the classroom that intelligent parents have dull children and unintelligent parents have brilliant children. But Jerman observed through tests of intelligence that 22.5 per cent of 62 top persons were related to 643 brilliant children*. This shows that heredity deeply affects intelligence.

(b) Another reason which brings forth the influence on intelligence is environment. Some children move frequently in the advanced social environment and consequently their level of intelligence is raised by interaction with the children of high I.Q. A case personally experienced can be cited in

*Tests were conducted in the University of California as indicated by Lindgren's book, *Educational Psychology in the Classroom* (Wiley International, 1972).

support of the above statement. Two sons of a wealthy businessman living in a native village of a rural environment got an opportunity for having their education in the metropolitan city of Bangalore. It was found after a decade that these two children of average intelligence in their native village showed extraordinary brilliance at Bangalore and both came out successfully to become IAS officers. Evidently this was the result of a congenial environment out of their village which affects mental growth. Thorndike is of the opinion that after studying in a supplicated educational institution of higher learning, pupils after some time score higher than students who get education in an ordinary institution. It is clear from the research that there is an increase undoubtedly in the scores in intelligence tests carried out after the children get the experience of urban public school education.

(c) If any child develops slowly, it must not be concluded that he is mentally inferior. Neither should it be assumed that if he develops rapidly he is mentally superior. A superior may be slow in getting started, and a dullard may make an impressive beginning (Figure 12.1).

The figure illustrates there patterns. Superior children do mature more frequently (1) and inferior more frequently like (3).

Note the differences becoming greater with increased chronological age. The backward or dull children are move inferior than the average as they get older and the superior child is more superior.

Figure 12.1

Mental Development of (1) Superior (2) Average, and (3) Dull Children

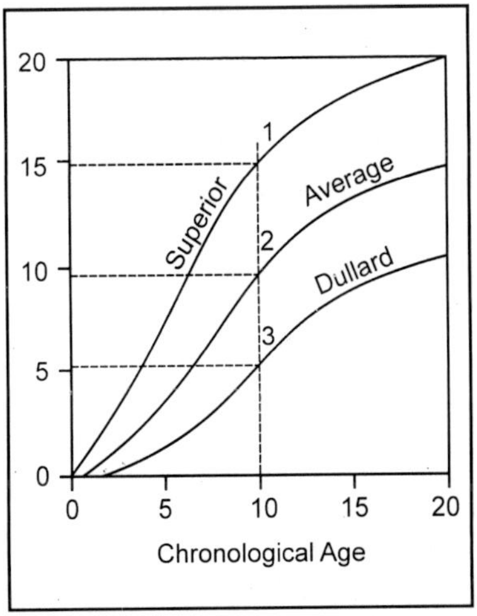

School and Classroom and Learner's Intelligence

Individual differences and variation in I.Q. of pupils in the classroom are the result of and responsibilities of schools where a teacher gives instructions according to individual capabilities. The teacher has to:

(i) Arrange for weekly/fortnightly tests and must have records of performance.

(ii) Provide adequate guidance to the children for showing regular increase in their abilities.

(iii) Provide a desirable environment for showing development in learning.

(iv) Employ devices for motivating pupils in accordance with their individual differences.

(v) Use flexible curriculum according to the needs and objectives. Pupils can take interest only when the teaching process is according to their needs.

(vi) Make use of materials and co-curricular activities like scouting, hiking, tours and travels and games.

(vii) Promote coordination between gifted and dullard children so that the latter may be able to get incentives and also the help of bright students.

(viii) Use methods of teaching which may prove useful and involve all pupils – bright, average and dullard. It is possible when the division in classes is in homogeneous groupings.

Intelligence Tests and Classroom Activities

It is necessary to test pupils and through their results, they are provided guidance by the teacher according to their strength or weakness. The most important use of tests in the class is to categorize pupils into average intelligence, below average or dull, and bright or having higher degrees than average.

A teacher must know the result of the teaching process and the missing links so that he may replan his lesson when he comes to know that some of the pupils have shown a lower level of intelligence. He should give extra time and efforts to make the pupils at par with the class. Similarly, when he is able to detect bright students, they should be provided useful opportunities to keep them apace with the advanced level of learning or learning material.

A teacher shuld be able to know and decipher problems of pupils. Tests can also help in this. They should identify delinquent children and provide guidance by measuring the level and the nature of delinquency. Tests can make surveys of the deaf, blind and slow learners. Teachers should administer the appropriate tests which may be different for different types of learners. Vocational and educational tests too differ. Therefore, the purpose for holding tests must be clear in the mind of the teacher. They should be very clear whether abstract ability is to be measured or social or motor ability is the motif to judge. A teacher has to decide which of the tests – Binet, Terman, Spearman or Thurston – would be beneficial to solve the problem.

Some salient characteristics would prove useful to understand these tests.

Types of Tests of Intelligence

Tests of intelligence are classified on the basis of the factors involved in the process of testing:

1. *One Single or Unit Factor:* Binet feels that intelligence can be described fully by one single factor, i.e., the ability to have good judgment. Terman also speaks of a single factor, i.e., ability to think conceptually. Some favour a factor known as the power of synthesis, i.e., to coordinate multiple impressions in a unitary whole.

   Single unit factor is criticized because intelligence cannot be measured by one single factor.

Figure 12.2

Showing Spearman's Two-Factor Concept of Intelligence

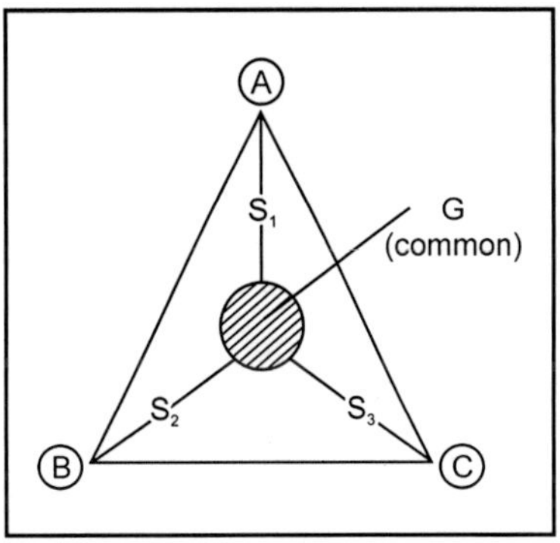

2. *Intelligence as a Two-Factor:* 'G' or general factor and 'S' as several specific factor. Spearman advocated that general factor plays some part in all human activities. There are also special types of activities which are associated with 'S' factor

There are several activities in which 'general' (G) plays a minor role. Therefore, Spearman included a group factor to the two factors. This can be shown by a simple diagram given below:

The diagram shows A,B,C as three tests. They are shaded by lines representing the element common to the group of tests. Unique part of each of three tests is shown by lincs S_1, S_2 and S_3. Thus common and specific, i.e., two factors, play a role.

3. *Three-Factor Concept:* E.L. Thorndike considered Spearman's two-factor concept as actually of three factors at the later stage. This is because of the fact that intellectual tasks are performed by a complex nervous system, and the two-factor notion is over-simplification. The intellectual task operates in different patterns.
4. *Multiple Factor Theory* holds that intelligence is made up of nine primary mental abilities, viz., (a) spatial, (b) perceptual, (c) numerical, (d) logical, (e) fluency of words, (f) memory, (g) inductive ability, (h) deductive ability, and (i) solution of a problem.
5. *Guilford Structure to Define Tasks or Tests:* Guilford opines that intellect is the organization of primary abilities into a structure of intellect. His notion is based on a 3D structure for each factor of process of operation, content and products.
   (i) *Process of operation* in five groups of mental abilities, i.e., (a) cognition, (b) memory, (c) convergent thinking, (d) divergent thinking, and (e) evaluation.
   (ii) *Content or material* comprises (a) figure content, (b) symbolic content, (c) semantic content, and (d) behavioural content.
   (iii) *Products* result from the application of operations to content. There are six categories, viz., (a) units, (b) classes, (c) relations, (d) systems, (e) transformations, and (f) implications. Each of the 15 cells is three-dimensional (3D) because in figures the interaction of three variations takes place, i.e., operation, content and products. Thus, there are five kinds of operations, four kinds of content, and six kinds of products, and thus, there are 5×4×6 = 120 cells. In this way, Guilford's notion about intelligence is the most comprehensive. It

has vast useful meaning for education. Students are not simply guided by stimulus-response and are not machine-like. They think variantly and present new ideas. Below is given a diagram showing Guilford's Structure of Memory and Thinking, which may be helpful to the teacher to practice in the classroom.

What do we infer from various types of intelligence tests? Various age groups and varied maturity-level pupils cannot be tested by homogenous methods. Intelligence tests measure the ability to learn, application of knowledge to new problems, perceiving relationship between activities and above all, the pupils' ability to reason. The teacher in his class holds these tests according to objectives of abilities. So it requires different types of tests

Figure 12.3

Guilford's Structure of Memory and Thinking

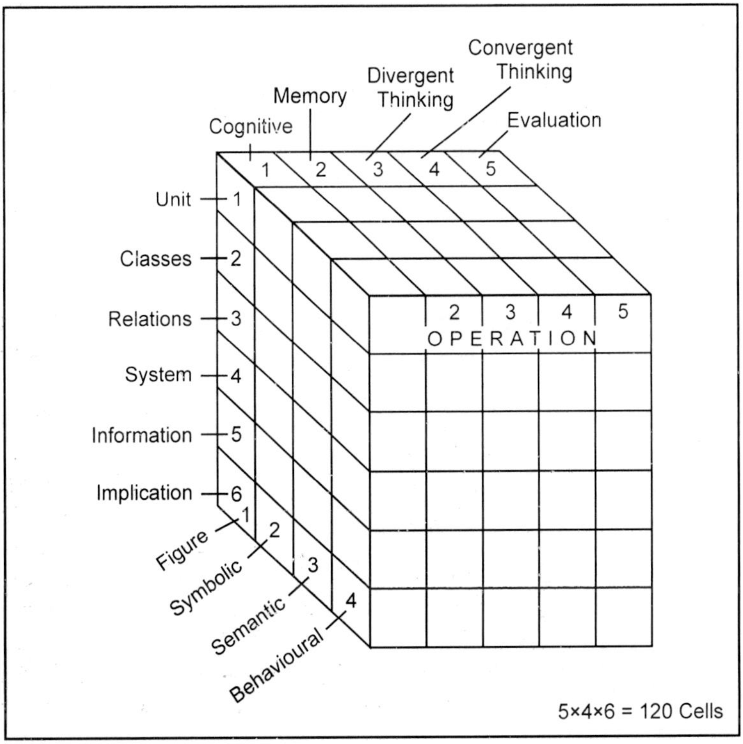

intermittently either for testing knowledge, power of reasoning or for the ability to solve the problem in hand. Gates and others favour pupils in the classroom to test simultaneously the abilities to learn, and to grasp facts both of abstract and concrete nature by mental control. This is only possible by the organization of abilities to develop ingenuity for solution of problems.

Application of Intelligence Tests in Education

A teacher knows the progress of his pupils through various tests held from time to time. Tests identify the level of knowledge imparted to pupils. They can be modified accordingly to situations, and therefore tests should be flexible. By knowing the level of knowledge imparted, the teacher modifies his teaching techniques. Tests are useful to provide adequate guidance. The superior pupils need extra opportunities for proper development.

Tests are also held to judge whether a student is capable of seeking admission for higher levels. They also help the teachers and experts to know the type of guidance – academic or vocational – the pupils of different channels need. Tests are also useful to identify the position in a particular job for pupils, i.e., secretarial, managerial or mechanical.

By achievement tests, the teacher can judge and identify differences in children's abilities. Therefore, the teacher should adopt a combination of teaching methods so that he may keep pace with the progress of all backward or bright pupils. Different children should be given different types of home assignments.

Education is not only for cognitive development. The motif of education is to face varied life situations. This needs coordination, cooperation and shouldering of responsibilities in schools. The teacher should take care of children by providing timely incentives for stimulating intellectual endeavour and for making proper social adjustment. In the classroom, motives are significant but their proper use is required at the proper moment. Gates opines that learning experiences prove useful only when these are coordinated to pupils' needs and interests. Incentives given to pupils are to contribute to their purpose and enable them to make more intelligent adjustments in the future.

QUESTIONS

Short Answer Type Questions

1. *Define*:
   (a) Motivation
   (b) Intelligence
   (c) Organization of Abilities
   (d) Mental Age
   (e) Intelligent Quotient.
2. *Discuss:*
   (a) Intelligence and mental powers
   (b) What is rational thinking?
   (c) I.Q. and individual differences
   (d) Classroom and individual variation in learning
   (e) Intelligence tests and classroom activities

Average Answer Type Questions

1. Types of intelligence tests
2. Guilford's structure of testing intelligence.
3. Application of intelligence tests in teaching

Essay Type Questions

1. Intelligence and Growth of Pupil
2. Measurement of Achievement in the Classroom
3. Classroom and Learner's Intelligence

References

Burt, C., 'The Development of Reasoning in Children', *Journal of Experimental Pedagogy*, Vol. 5, Nos 2–3, 1919, pp. 121–27.

Cattle, R.B., *Guide to Mental Testing*, University of London Press, London, 1948.

Freeman, F.S., *Individual Differences: The Nature and Causes of Variation in Intelligence and Special Abilities*, Henry Holt, N.Y., 1934.

Goddard, G.D., *The Meaning of Intelligence*, Macmillan, NY, 1943.

Piaget, J., *Psychology of Intelligence*, Harcourt, NY, 1930.

Pressey, S.L. and F.P. Robinson, *Psychology and the New Education*, Harper, NY, 1944.

Terman, L.M. and M.A. Merill, *Measuring of Intelligence*, Houghton-Mifflin, Boston, 1937.

Thorndike, E.L., *Human Learning*, The Century Co., N.Y., 1931.

Thurstone, L.L., *Primary Mental Abilities*, University of Chicago Press, Chicago, 1938.

Part IV

Exceptional Children and Classroom Teaching

13

Teaching Process of the Talented and Gifted Children

Who are Exceptional Children?

Children who perform above average and possess, I.Q. more than 140 are known as talented or gifted. Samuel A. Kirk defines 'exceptional' as a high quality of children who deviate from the normal in mental, physical and social characteristics. They require special educational services to develop to their maximum capacity. The future of any country depends much on the maximum number of school-going children possessing creativity. Creative people are extra intelligent and hold responsible positions in the society. They can be scientific, academic and artistic. Their number must be regularly increased by providing essential facilities for their special type of education.

Talented or gifted is not the only class of exceptional children. There are several classes of exceptional population of school-going children. The classes include (a) gifted or talented, (b) mentally backward, (c) physically-handicapped, and (d) delinquent or problem children. Generally, it is found that classes of exceptional children form more than 75 per cent of school-going children and they are either above the average or below the average class of children. The following graph represents three broad categories: (1) average, (2) negative exceptional, and (3) positive exceptional. Negative and positive are further divided into four sub-classes each ranging between 0 and 100 as A, B, C and D. The graph represents the number of children generally found in the school classroom. The number indicates that nearly 50 per cent of the school-going children are of average intelligence. They are neither talented, nor they are backward. They sometimes show average results, but below the level. Similarly, some of them are of average standard, but above the level. The role of the teacher is to motivate them to make progress and rise to the positive level of either superior or higher level than average.

Figure 13.1

Normal Distribution of Classes of School-going Pupils

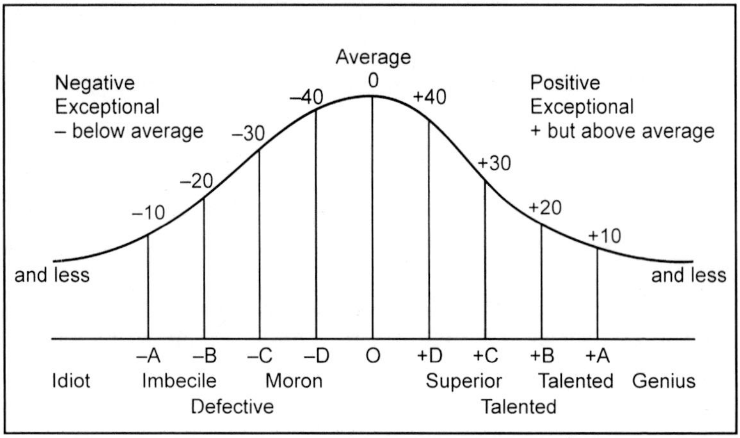

Nearly 10 per cent or even less than 10 are children showing either level known as idiot and nearly the same number of children as gifted or talented. The teacher has to make special arrangements for guiding them. The talented should be reinforced and further motivated to refine the skills they possess. The idiots may be given strenuous practice to raise the level of their understanding and consequently, may fall into the category of positive average.

In this chapter, we discuss talented or gifted children and their educational process.

Who are Gifted or Talented Children?

Gifted or talented students possess several types of abilities and skills such as intellectual, scientific, leadership, creative, artistic, mechanical, and physical. Therefore, the teacher should make a careful observation to identify the student's behaviour to classify him in a group of particular skills. Talent can be displayed in one or the several skills mentioned above. Classroom teaching is more concerned with the intellectual skill and behavioural traits of pupil to adjust with the new situation with care. This depends much on heredity as well as environment of the pupil both in school as well as at home. Before going into the several causes responsible for causing or developing talents or skills, it is better to define the meaning of talent.

Meaning of Talent of Children in School and Classroom

In the classroom talented children are identified through their level of intelligence. The level is measured by several tests conducted by the teacher in the classroom. Usually a teacher tries to identify the performance of a child in the classroom by nature of expression – written and oral – and about the problem raised. The talented child shows special abilities in dealing with the problem raised for him or her through intelligence of superior level or above the average level. The number of such students who have much higher level than common pupils varies from school to school and also from country to country. Their number depends both on heredity as well as on the environment of the school and also of the outside world.

In the classroom students display various types of abilities. Some are having high order of intellectual ability, while there are a few who possess scientific and creative ability. Some students show a quality of leadership, while a few show talent in music, drama, painting or even in writing stories, poems or essays on current problems. There are students in the class who possess mechanical skills. It is not uncommon to come across pupils in the classroom who score high in games and athletics activities, including hiking, camping, swimming, shooting, etc.

So, pupils in the classroom show talent either in a single field or in multifarious activities. The role of the teacher is very critical to judge talent or talents in his students. This requires patience. Only tests or examination are not the only criteria to identify talent.

Definitions of Talented or Gifted Children

Many definitions are available for gifted children. Most of the psychologists agree that the children having an I.Q. more than 130 are usually known as gifted. In a school, generally the percentage of talented children varies between 2–5.

Samuel A. Kirk says a gifted child may possess any of the abilities among social, mechanical, artistic, musical, linguistic, physical or academic.

The National Society for the Study of Education defines a gifted child as "one who shows consistently remarkable performance in any worthwhile line of endeavour".

Tyler defines a gifted child as one who is exceptional in the amount of his production rate and quality of his production.

Kolsenik defines every child as talented who in his group is superior in some ability which makes his an outstanding contribution to the welfare and quality living in our society.

Gallaghar identifies exceptionally capable learners as individuals having in common the ability to absorb abstract concepts, to organize them more effectively and to apply them more appropriately than those who are not so capable.

Lewis M. Terman found that gifted children are more active and energetic than average-level children. They generally have an I.Q. of 140 or more. Most of them are educationally advanced beyond the average grade status for their ages.

Characteristics of Gifted Children

Gifted children may perform excellently either in single or multiple sectors. This has been already pointed out that the various sectors in which students may depict abilities of extraordinary quality include intellectual, scientific, leadership, creative, artistic, writing, dramatic, musical, mechanical and physical skills. The following are given important points of various sectors as characteristics to identify students as gifted:

1. *Intellectual ability* includes that he or she:
   (a) learns rapidly with ease and comfort
   (b) possesses common sense and practical knowledge
   (c) shows power of reasoning clearly and identifies relationships to understand meanings

(d) shows power of retaining knowledge without drill

(e) knows about many things of which many students are unaware

(f) has in memory a large vocabulary to use appropriately

(g) has a taste for reading books other than class text, in advance of the other students

(h) shows mental ability to perform difficult tasks

(i) has the ability to interact and to ask questions showing varied interests

(j) has the capacity to handle academic assignments such as reports, minutes of meetings, drafting courses of instructions, summarizing lectures of the class teacher, etc.

(k) can think original ideas and can interpret situations in their real perspectives.

In the classroom, a student who is intellectually gifted can be judged by the teacher's own standard tests and by the cumulative records maintained by the teacher.

2. *Scientific ability of a gifted child:*

 (a) He possesses a clear and accurate expression about abstract concepts and ideas related to natural phenomena.

 (b) He shows extra taste for the mathematical process to deal with problems.

 (c) He possesses better coordination of hands, head and eyes to perform projects and mechanical tasks accurately and systematically.

 (d) He is fond of experiments and does not feel bored with the complicated process.

 (e) He takes a lot of interest in constructing and repairing domestic articles such as a watch, radio, electric-short circuit and ordinary water tapes, rain gauge, telescope, etc.

 (f) He reads scientific literature with understanding and discusses objectively.

3. Besides the two major sectors listed above, a gifted child may show the ability of leadership in various fields such as sport, polities, social meetings, art and music, group activities, etc.

Role of Teachers in Guiding Gifted Children

Teachers must be careful about gifted children and see that they adjust comfortably with the typical school situation. They should arrange special classes. Gifted children need training to mix up with pupils who are less able.

The teacher should take extra note of the gifted children because they often behave negatively and are restless, lazy, inattentive and can create disturbance. They also find the school curriculum unchallenging and stale. Usually they become uninterested in the usual routine class work. Their egoistic behaviour and outspoken nature become a problem for the teacher. These activities should be curbed by providing them opportunities of their standard, to make them active in the class routine. This may be done by assigning them home tasks in the form of projects: drafting of projects, preparation of learning material and suggesting objectives related to advanced and newer methodology of instruction. It is very necessary to keep their mental equilibrium according to their challenging traits of behaviour.

The teacher should not feel hesitant in suggesting hobbies for the gifted. A day may be fixed fortnightly to allow a gifted child to show his or her talent by holding meetings, seminars and also providing an opportunity for taking teaching work. The teacher may provide advanced and enriched material to analyse, summarize and to express the substance before the entire class.

E. Paul Torrence (1962) advanced certain activities to make gifted children busy with the work of their level and taste. He suggested that they should be motivated more and more to environmental stimuli and taught to test each idea systematically. A teacher should not force them toward a set pattern, rather they should be encouraged to tolerate new ideas and self-initiated learning. The gifted children should be provided opportunities to manipulate materials, ideas, concepts, tools and structures. They should be encouraged to consider problems as a whole and to emphasize on complete structures.

Torrence also suggested certain principles for teachers to make children advanced in thinking above the average group. The teacher should:

(a) Recognize and acknowledge potentialities of children through various types of tests

(b) Show respect for interaction, i.e., questioning and responding to express new ideas.

(c) Teacher may motivate children by asking provocative questions

(d) Teacher should provide opportunities for original thinking

(e) Teacher may promote planned experiences and experiments

(f) Teacher may create problems which can be solved by adequate skills and library research

QUESTIONS

Short Answer Type Questions

1. *Define*:

    (a) Interaction

    (b) Creativity

    (c) Exceptional Children

    (d) Mental Age

    (e) Idiot

    (f) Scientific Talent

    (g) Divergent Ideas

    (h) Provocative Questions

2. What are several categories of exceptional children?

3. What do you mean by negative exceptional children?

Average Answer Type Questions

1. Discuss the characteristics of intellectually gifted children.

2. Classify and show graphically exceptional children.

3. Give chief characteristics to identify school-going talented children.

4. Discuss a teacher's responsibilities to develop qualities essential for the pupils to qualify to be included in a group of gifted ones.

Essay Type Questions

1. Talented or gifted children
2. Classroom activities suitable for talented pupils
3. Teacher's role toward gifted children in a classroom.

References

Abraham, W., *A Guide for the Study of Exceptional Children*, Sergeant, Boston, 1956.

Gallagher, James J., *Teaching the Gifted Child*, 2nd Edition, Allyn and Bacon, Boston, 1975.

Gassel, A.L., *Genius Giftedness and Growth and Studies in Child Development*, Harper, NY, 1948.

Kirk, Samuel A., *Educating Exceptional Children*, Oxford, New Delhi, 1963.

Terman, L.M., *Genetic Studies of Genius*, Stanford University Press, California, 1925.

Torrence, E. Paul, *Revarding Creative Behaviour*, Prentice Hall, N.Y., 1965.

14

Mentally Retarded or Backward Pupils and their Educational Process

An authoritative book *Backward Child* has been written by Cyril Burt. In the book, several symptoms, causes and their remedies have been discussed. According to Burt, a backward child in his or her class is unable to do the normal work, and normally his performance is below average for his age. He or she is also unable to take those advantages from the process of teaching which are availed by other normal pupils of the class.

The mental level of the backward child is below average. A precise definition, therefore, is given in terms of 'Educational Quotient'. It is calculated by an average of mental ages of different subjects in the classroom, divided by the chronological age of the child concerned and multiplied by 100. Suppose the mental age of the child in the class is 10 and chronological age is 12, then EQ = $10/12 \times 100 = 83.3$ or in whole number as 83. According to Burt, a child whose EQ is below 85 is known as a backward child.

Generally, backward children are considered a problem in the class. But a careful teacher tries to investigate the causes of backwardness of the child. He may be backward in studies because of his low level of mental abilities. Low mental abilities may be due to auditory or visual defects, or some physical disabilities. He must not be neglected and the teacher should give due consideration to physical deficiencies. There may be external causes related to family circumstances or due to environmental affiliations such as company of bad friends. The teacher may consult for external causes either with parents of children, or their close friends. He takes steps to keep the child off the bad company of friends.

Types of Backwardness

Environmental Backwardness

This is a common cause of backwardness of children in the classroom. A child may be from the rural sector and also may economically belong to a poor family. The teacher may help him by providing books and also the required physical aids like tuition fees, etc., as well as nourishment during the school period. Above all, the child should be given sympathetic treatment. The bad company of a child may be made defunct gradually by assigning the child projects of his taste, keeping him busy with games of his interest and by their participation in other co-curricular activities. The serious cases may be referred to the family members of the child to deal with adequacy and intelligence.

Being backward in class is no serious defect. A backward child needs proper guidance and constant practical exercises to practice. He needs problems from simple to complex, easy to difficult and from life-bound to conceptual to deal with. He should be given an environment in the class which is somewhat related to his hobbies, to play or in games of his interest. He may be kept busy by providing current issues and lively problems of home and neighbourhood.

Backwardness of pupils in the class is much due to defective teaching and also by teaching the ill-organized syllabi. The courses should not be unplanned and be not too ambitious for the pupils' mental level. A few students because of their parents' over-ambitions get admitted in inadequate standards. They have to face difficulties and gradually lag behind in the class.

Some of the students because of some unavoidable reasons remain regularly absent from their classes, and they turn backward in their courses of teaching. They are unable to cope with the current topics related to the knowledge of previous courses. The school mismanagement coupled with poor teaching methodology make pupils disinterested and they become backward in the process of learning. Backwardness due to environmental situations of pupils in the class may be checked by keeping pupils engaged in co-curricular activities both at home and in the school.

Backwardness Due to Sensory Defects

This may be called a special type of physical defect. Backwardness in reading, writing and answering about a problem raised by the teacher may be due to poor hearing, defective visual perception and inattentiveness in the class. Such students need special care by the teacher. They should be given proper seats, especially in the first two rows in the class. Serious cases may be referred to the specialist and their parents should also be informed to take necessary steps. Students who are suffering from sensory defects need sympathy by the teacher as well as by classmates. They should not be ridiculed.

Backwardness Due to Physical Defects

Physical causes make children backward in their classes and pupils generally remain backward in the process of learning as compared to other average pupils. The sufferers need sympathy of teachers and parents. They should be made at par with other average pupils by means of love and affection. They need security and to look forward for attending to their problems. If these are not met sympathetically, they feel nervous and become disturbed emotionally. This makes them backward in their achievements and they lag behind in knowledge and understanding as compared with the average pupils. Their Educational Quotient also gradually falls and they remain immature because they are unable to pick up the level of intelligence of their physical age.

Mentally Retarded Children

They generally show backwardness because of their ill-temperament. According to Burt, nearly 9 per cent of pupils in a class of 50 suffer from mentally poor performance because they possess low intelligence and are found psychologically disturbed. The area of their mental structure is defective and their low Educational Quotient (EQ) and their poor attitude make their performance lower than the average. They also possess lesser capacity than their other classmates in conceptual understanding. They are unable to correlate various experiences to solve the problem. Their power of reasoning is poor.

Mentally-retarded children need special training, and they should be taught practical aspects rather than verbal expression. They should be kept mentally alert by assigning them topics of their interest to prepare charts and to make them coordinate with the projects. Their mental backwardness may be checked by keeping them engaged in group activities like games and sports, scouting, social services, NCC, etc. Mentally-retarded children need not be taught separately. But they need more and more opportunities to work cooperatively with a group of four-five pupils. They are required to complete their assignment, which must be of different nature from the rest of the pupils.

Backwardness Due to Learning Difficulties

The Neurology World Federation defines difficulty in learning to read by the word 'Dyslexia'. This is a heredity backwardness and some children are born with dyslexia, which means 'underachievement in writing and reading skills'. Children who suffer from this disease have problems with reading with accuracy, speed and comprehension. They also commit errors in spellings, and it is found that they have an illegible handwriting.

Dyslexia is not a disease and needs no doctor business. It is a product of a special kind of mental poverty. Many well-known personalities have had deficiency of illegible writing and underachievement in writing and reading.

The problem needs a proper diagnostic process both by parents and also by teachers to bring the sufferers in the line of an average reader or writer. The past history of the family may be traced to find the relevant causes. The best remedial measure is intensive practice and to encourage the sufferers to begin to write with words joined together.

Education for Backward Children

There are three different ways of providing education to backward pupils. They should be taught either by holding separate classes for them in the same school or they should be taught along with other pupils in one and the same regular period. The third alternative is that a special school for backward pupils be arranged to provide them special training.

(a) The backward pupils who are taught with the normal pupils in a regular class face several difficulties to cope with the situations of learning because the education quotients of both the categories differ. The backwards many gradually face further difficulty and stand at the lowest order. It is also possible that they prove to be a hindrance in the growth of normal students. It is not sensible and worthwhile to teach both the categories with the same and evenly planned methodology.

The practice of teaching backward and normal pupils together is possible only when the teacher adopts some special types of creative methods and provides separate exercises and projects to backward pupils. They may be encouraged to complete the creative exercises in cooperation with the pupils of higher intelligence.

(b) Another device suggested is to hold special classes in the same school for the pupils who are below average, or backward. The teacher may identify children with EQ ranging from 50 to 75 and provide them special coaching through special instructions, and giving them working exercises which may gradually remove the deficiencies.

Special classes need extra time, which may be arranged either before or after the regular hours of the school. It is also essential that special teachers are appointed for this purpose. The special classes save the backward pupils from undesirable competition or from developing an inferiority complex. The special teacher has to understand and classify several types of needs and problems. He has enough time and scope to guide the backward students in their creative work, projects and experiments.

(c) The third alternative is to provide the backward pupils a separate class in a separate special school. The special school has a different type of environment. It is equipped with special equipment, laboratory and paraphernalia for guiding students. This type of school is an expensive venture and an affair too costly to accommodate. The separate environment is also a negative factor and pupils are unable to be motivated by world affairs.

Role of Teachers in Ameliorating the Pupils' Backwardness

In a classroom, a teacher must follow steps from simple to complex, from known to unknown and from concrete to abstract.

The goals and objectives should be clear and related to life-bound experiences. Practically, the objectives must be achievable during the course of teaching.

The given material should not be jumbled or overloaded by unknown facts. These may be simple to retain, and also related to pupils' interest.

The backward pupils need motivation to learn new experiences. Motivation is provided through varied means – pictures, charts, films, praise and reward.

The pupils should be engaged to perform activities through their mental capacities. The material which is to be provided should be meaningful and helpful in removing difficulties.

The pupils may be made aware of their result of achievement immediately so that the feedback is received for further improvement and for repetition, or to provide a task of some different nature.

The teacher must inform the parents about the difficulties of their children, who are unable to achieve as much knowledge as a normal child can. The teacher may regularly keep the parents informed about the progress of the backward children through various types of tests. The teacher can assess the progress through the result of the tests and can know the problems to understand the reasons for the difficulty in adjusting with the average group. The mentally retarded group of pupils needs sympathetic treatment both at home and in the classroom. The teacher has to show a lot of patience and make constant painstaking efforts. They should be taught simple vocabulary.

Remedial Measures to Remove General Backwardness

Diagnose the defects of the backward child, and if necessary, take help of a medical doctor to identify physical defects. The physically backward child needs amelioration of physically disabilities.

A mentally-retarded child generally remains below the level of average in studies. He or she needs special coaching practice as has been already discussed previously.

Most of the children are backward because they are unable to get a favourable and congenial home environment, and many of them do not get education in good schools. These backward children need a favourable, sympathetic and affectionate environment both at home and school. They should be given opportunities to get admission in a good public school where teaching is available for their varied interests, hobbies and constructive activities. The methods of teaching should also be coupled with projects and practical exercises, including experiments.

Backward pupils feel exhilarated if they are taught with the help of visual aids and more through self-activities, experiments, etc. They should be assigned projects, art and painting work, etc., and they may be kept busy also through recitation, dramatics and play. Some of the students run away from their classes because the teaching process is beyond their level of understanding and does not appeal to them, being dry, full of facts and based on textbooks. The teacher should make all efforts to stop them from missing classes through introducing various types of creative assignments to complete in the class itself in coordination with others. The cases of truancy should be carefully dealt with.

A child may be backward in only one or two subjects. For example, the general case is that students are weak and backward in Mathematics. Many are weak in English. Such cases may specially be treated by the teacher, and individually they should be made to practise to follow steps, and to apply each formula with comprehension. The teacher should proceed with a logical sequence to make the difficulties removed with patience and should not skip over the difficulties. The best way to remove the general backwardness is to attach the backward pupils with an intelligent group to take care regularly.

Intelligence Quotient of Mentally-Retarded Children

Mentally-retarded children are those who generally possess an IQ below 70. The teacher may inform the parents that their children are not performing satisfactorily and they are mentally deviated. It is the duty of a responsible teacher to educate the parents about the normal mental caliber of their children. But, the parents should also be taught to relieve their children from undue force or pressure which causes tension. It causes many emotional problems and their adjustment with the normal working of the school becomes a difficult task. A mentally-retarded child needs sympathy and timely motivation. If he is forcibly admitted to a school of higher level, he will show a poor performance. He will not be able to compete with his classmates. Therefore, it is necessary that mentally-retarded children are given proper sympathetic treatment in school. They should be taught simple vocabulary by a series of pictorial stories. The reading material should also be of their interest.

Children whose IQ is below 50 should be placed in special coaching schools where special instructors provide them training. The American Association of Mental Deficiency (AAMD) classifies retarded children into three categories: mild (IQ between 67–52), moderate (between 51–36) and severe retardation (IQ 19 and below).

Slow Learners

Between an average learner and retarded children, there is one more category known as 'slow learner'. Slow learners are not handicapped and they are also not retarded. The main characteristics of slow learners are:

(a) immature as compared to their mental age,
(b) they often show mental frustration because they are unable to perform equally all things which are done by an average group in their class,
(c) possess a tendency of self-devaluation, and
(d) lack confidence.

Teachers can improve slow learners by motivating them through easy situations and smooth solutions to problems. This may not breed frustration in the slow learners. Only those assignments are given to them which they can complete with ease. It is necessary to reinforce their responses to create in them confidence and a sense of self-esteem. The teacher may assign them brief lessons to learn and to complete within a short duration of time. They should not be over-taxed. It is necessary to teach them in well-coordinated steps and also in series with previously-learnt lessons. In other words, programmed instructions are useful for slow learners.

QUESTIONS

Short Answer Type Questions

1. *Define:*
   (a) Mentally-retarded Child
   (b) Backward Physically
   (c) Environmental Backwardness
   (d) Educational Quotient
   (e) Sensory Defects of Child
   (f) Classroom Environment
   (g) Dyslexic Child

Average Answer Type Questions

1. Distinguish between children who are backward and slow learners.
2. What are the causes for the backwardness of pupils in the classroom?
3. Give characteristics of a backward child.
4. Explain exceptional children.
5. Write briefly about the remedial measures which should be adopted by a teacher to bring a backward child into a line of common abilities child.
6. How should a teacher guide a backward child?

Essay Type Questions

1. Classroom Activities and Backward Children
2. General Backwardness versus Special Backwardness
3. Teaching Process and Backwardness of Pupils

References

Anastasi, A., *Psychological Testing*, Macmillan, NY, 1965.

Bernard, H.W., *Mental Hygiene for Classroom Teachers*, McGraw-Hill, NY, 1952.

——, *Psychology of Learning and Teaching*, McGraw-Hill, NY, 1972.

Bloom, B.S., *Taxonomy of Educational Objectives*, Longmans, NY, 1965.

Bugelski, B.R., *Learning and Motivation*, Henry Holt, NY, 1956.

Burt, C., *The Backward Child*, London University Press, London, 1937.

Chaubey, S.P., *Developmental Psychology*, N. Agarwal & Sons, Agra, 1976.

Crow, L.D. and A. Crow, *Mental Hygiene*, McGraw-Hill, NY, 1951.

Heck, A.O., *Education for Exceptional Children*, McGraw-Hill, NY, 1940.

Lindgren, H.C., *Educational Psychology in the Classroom*, Wiley International, NY, 1972.

Peters, M., *Diagnostic and Remedial Spelling Manual*, Macmillan, NY, 1975.

Sarason, S., *Psychological Problems in Mental Deficiency*, Harper, NY, 1953.

Thurstone, L.L., *Primary Mental Abilities*, Chicago University Press, Chicago, 1938.

15

Handicapped and Delinquent Children and Problems for their Classroom Teaching Practice

The previous chapter has given a vivid account of the various categories of children who are either above average or below average mentally. They are known as gifted or backward, and their cases are exceptionally different from the children who are normal in their performances.

There is another section of exceptional qualities which is known as the category of children who are physically abnormal and generally called as 'handicapped'. Besides the handicapped who are normal except for their physical defect, there is one more category of exceptional children who are delinquent and are harmful for our society and the country's progress. These children are called 'delinquent' because their behaviour is generally against social norms.

In the present chapter, an effort has been made to discuss the problems of handicapped and delinquent children, and the role of the teacher to tackle with them in the classroom. Let us take the case of the handicapped.

Who are 'Handicapped'?

A child who is physically abnormal and suffers from impairment inhibiting him from participating in normal activities is called handicapped. Some children have a defect in their body by birth or they may be handicapped due to some accident. The physical impairment may be serious or simple. But, the impairment adversely affects the education of a child. UNESCO celebrates the 'Child Year' which showers the right of living successfully, and this is possible only when each child receives education successfully.

Handicapped children must get their due education to contribute in the development of society and country. This is only possible when there is proper arrangement in the country for their education. They need special types of schools with special provisions of equipment and specially-trained teachers. In India, it is a matter of deep concern that there is a paucity of institutions for the handicapped. Whatever is available, it is very nominal and not up to the mark.

Problems for Handicapped

The handicapped children in school face numerous difficulties in adjustment with the activities because of physical deformities. They are unable to perform normal duties and are forced to substitute their interest. Therefore, they become emotionally disturbed and their mental level too is adversely affected. Naturally, there develops a sort of inferiority complex in the children and they often display resentment because of the unfulfilment of certain assignments successfully or at par with the normal classmates. It is for these problems that the handicapped children need special attention from teachers and also from parents.

The handicapped child develops a feeling of self-debasement because of physical inabilities. This feeling consequently causes in the disabled child an attitude of helplessness for attaining proper adjustment. Such children need a favourable environment in school and at home. It is generally seen that handicapped children are not weak mentally. If they are kept for months together in an advanced school with a congenial environment, they show good results. In a good public school atmosphere, the handicapped children can explore their intelligence fully to compensate for the physical disability.

Education for Physically Handicapped

Children who are physically challenged may not be weak mentally and therefore, they should not be refrained from participating in all classroom activities irrespective of their physical impairment. Impetus may be provided to them by giving opportunities to join vocational training such as shorthand and type-writing practice, banking and insurance service coaching and accountancy, management, etc. It may be carefully observed that they are able to carry on with their assigned work satisfactorily despite their physical disability. The job in their life may develop in them confidence and self-respect and they may easily seek independent thinking for adjustment with life situations.

The teacher may provide handicapped children education through special schools where they get all required facilities to show their worth. The special school can provide the handicapped children with adequate seating arrangement in accordance with their physical comfort and an environment suitable to them for development.

The teacher may provide assistance to the handicapped child through school doctor's advice and may ask the parents to get them examined from time to time. Handicapped children need sympathetic behaviour from the co-workers, parents and other members of the locality. This is necessary to make them realize their importance in society. They should not be considered inferior than others.

The teacher should take extra care for supplying the required material to the handicapped suffering from visual or hearing defects. The courses and books, etc., should also be planned specially to suit their objectives. Some of the handicapped are physically weak. They should be provided nourished food, milk, etc., during the interval time in schools. The parents should also be informed to take care of their health and weak organs of the body. Cleanliness and care must be fully adhered too.

Types of Handicapped Children and Role of Teachers

(1) Crippled children in the class suffer generally because of their deformed organs which prevent them from working with normal capacity. Their muscles and joints are not in order. The crippled are superior in performance as far as their mental achievements are

concerned provided they get proper training and opportunities to show their worth. Often the crippled learn quickly and make adjustment with their situation by practice. Education by means of proper equipment and special training are like a bonus. These change their attitude and they are able to adjust to their deformities in due time.

It is not desirable psychologically that crippled children are placed in a separate school because the idea of aloofness might adversely affect their social adjustment. But the space or room for training must be special where they can work with ease and can also have opportunities for get-togethers.

Vocational training is a boon to the crippled pupils and it is reformatory in the course of their progress. As far as possible, they should be placed in sedentary jobs for showing their capabilities fully.

(2) Children suffering from blindness or who are near blind have to be dealt with very carefully by their teachers. It is of utmost and urgent need that their defects are identified in the classroom for early treatment. Generally it is seen that some children who are not having normal vision feel difficulty in taking notes or to draw figures from the blackboard. They are also unable to read correctly and with normal speed. Blinking while reading or holding the book very near to eyes or in a peculiar way are some of the symptoms of near blindness. They need treatment at the earliest and should be referred to a doctor for examining and testing to suggest proper remedial measures.

The children suffering from total blindness must be admitted to a special school. There are adequate facilities provided for the blind and proper training is given to them for the appropriate vocation.

It is generally found that cases of children suffering from blindness and near blindness are handled in two different ways:

(a) Near-blind cases or children suffering from short-sightedness may be referred to doctors and their parents should be informed. These cases need to be attended to without any loss of time, otherwise the trouble may be turned into incurable and the pupils may become unfit to attend the classes.

    Those children who suffer from partial short-sightedness may be shifted to special coaching classes. These classes are equipped with adequate light facilities. Children are also provided with special books with bold printed matter. The blackboard should be properly coloured, neatly visible and kept at the right distance.

(b) Total-blind children, as suggested above, need to be admitted to special schools meant for the Braille system of education and should be given training for vocational adjustment. A blind child may also be taught to sing or to learn some form of handicraft.

The teacher in general schools should pay extra attention towards the prevention of eye defects. Eye defects are caused primarily by the inadequate environmental influences that weaken the eyesight. It is advisable to use spectacles or glasses as per the advice of a doctor. Besides this, the classroom should be equipped with adequate lighting facilities. Bold printed books may also prove useful.

(c) Deaf and hard-of-hearing children suffer from hearing clearly and correctly because they have lost their hearing power before they achieve speech or they have lost hearing after learning to speak. It is very necessary to make proper adjustment with these children. It is possible through the symbolic system of education for them to be able to communicate with normal people.

The task for educating the deaf and dumb is not easy and it is not possible to carry on with the usual types of schools. Special schools are required to cope with the situation. Helen Keller is remembered for her achievements. She was both deaf and blind but she could get the highest order of skill of communication. Her technique has become popular and people in various sectors are doing their job satisfactorily. Deaf and dumb individuals should be given enough opportunities for making contacts with the outside world. They may gradually pick up some viable means to communicate with persons of various sectors.

Hard-of-hearing children may be taught in schools with regular students. They may be given seats in first two rows of the class so that they may imitate the teacher's style of lip movement to pick up meanings. They should be gradually given training to study lip reading, and through practice they can pick up speech correctly.

(d) Children with speech defect are also identified as handicapped because their progress of learning is below average. Their performance is not satisfactory because they converse with stammering, and nasally. Generally, their defective speech is known as 'baby talk'. This defect is largely due to physiological reasons, and psychological too. Habitually, there are certain children who find pleasure in speaking or frittering meaninglessly. Later on, they are identified as handicapped because of being defective in speech, the reasons being carelessness and imitation of faulty speech, emotional disturbances and lack of affection or proper peace, rest, etc.

Pupils suffering from defective speech cannot recite properly and they fail utterly in reciting poems or telling stories impressively. The teacher can try to make them good narrators through certain steps as:

(a) Providing opportunities regularly for imitating good speech and recitation of poems, etc.

(b) Teacher may ask their parents to keep the home environment tension-free and peaceful.

(c) School work and home assignments may be light and simple. There should not be undue force on such children about school work and punishment.

(d) Proper nourishment is very essential to be given during school time.

(e) Some sort of training or speech delivering practice is useful.

Delinquent Children

What is Delinquency?

Delinquency is not a chronic disease. It is simply a mental derailment caused by several factors distorting an individual's personality. It affects human behaviour negatively, and it is therefore considered anti-social and harmful for the social culture. Delinquent children are the ones who deviate from the norms and ideals of society. A step further, Cyril Burt points out that a child is technically delinquent when he or she behaves against the social norms to the extent of becoming a subject of official action.

Delinquent children are emotionally maladjusted and are unable to solve problems. Gradually they become a menace to the peace and security of the society. A delinquent child is normally unable to fulfil his physical and social needs, and his personality is distorted. A delinquent individual remains neglected and suffers from a lack of belongingness. It is painful that be does not get opportunities to participate in common activities with the children of his age group because of his troublesome attitude and maladjusted behaviour.

Causes of Delinquency

Delinquency is not innate and no child is delinquent by birth. But most of the cases of delinquency are related to family circumstances, and gradually their environmental disequilibrium makes the children maladjusted. Naturally there are several factors responsible for mental disorder and maladjustment which are related both to the family circumstances and also to the adverse environment of the sufferer.

In a family, some children may get certain delinquent tendencies from heredity or parents' diseases. For example, low I.Q. of parents follows to their offspring and consequently their bad habits help to encourage delinquent behaviour. Poverty in the family also affects the child who may develop anti-social behaviour and suffers from habits like theft, telling lies, picking up quarrels, etc. Poverty of the family generates dejection, frustration and revolt in the minds of children. They are unable to make adjustments both at home and school and the outside world.

There are also certain families where parents, especially mothers, are engaged in work outside. The children of these families remain neglected and lack proper care. It generates anti-social behaviour in children. In some families parents generally quarrel on grounds which children fail to understand. They become unhappy, dejected and maladjusted. The presence of a stepmother in the family is an obvious cause to disturb the children mentally. They gradually become anti-social and maladjusted.

Physical health of children can also lead to delinquency. These include physical deformities, glandular defects or slow or unusually fast growth. An ugly face and deformed organs or some such physical abnormalities develop in children the feeling of inferiority and also a mental complex, which is looked down upon by others. It causes delinquency and anti-social behaviour. There is also possibility of the development of false self-pride, which may cause a distorted personality and in future such children may turn abnormal and anti-social. Grown-up children of about 14–15 years of age get the sex urge. If they are not dealt with properly due to family circumstances, they become maladjusted and some of them commit suicide or anti-social activities.

In schools and classrooms, lack of recreational facilities and co-curricular activities may also cause maladjustment. The company of bad friends, drunkards or gamblers may adversely affect the normal growth of children, and they may develop delinquent behaviour. In the classroom, the teacher's behaviour should not be discriminatory or partial towards any special child. This makes others begin to revolt in the class and their anti-social activities disturb the normal routine and the teaching process.

Remedial Measures to Check Delinquency

It is certain that no child is delinquent when born. It results mainly due to critical family circumstances and environmental conditions of school children. Children become delinquent because of the grave conditions and total negligence of members of the family. Therefore, delinquent behaviour may be checked by proper care, sympathy, affection and love of the family members. Parents must take timely steps to check abnormal behaviour of their children. They can provide essential necessities out of their limited sources of income. They can also let the children know about the paucity of economic resources and limited budget available for each of the members. The child may sympathetically begin to understand the critical situation. He or she should be satisfied that only the legitimate desire can be fulfilled.

When a child in the family takes note that all the members get things according to their abilities, there is no cause of his revolt against the society. Ambitions and expectations beyond capacities are generally not fulfilled, and the child must be taught the reality in school. The teacher may infuse in children that an easy and normal life without undue tensions can be happily passed only by following the dictum – 'the truth, beauty and good'. It is necessary to check dissatisfaction of the family members, and it is the duty of elders to teach ideals of life. At the same time, it is the duty of school teachers to train children to get adjusted in the circumstances where poverty and social inequality prevail.

Another aspect of children's delinquent behaviour is environmental. There may be enough chances that a child picks up abnormal behaviour because of the bad company of friends or classmates. In such circumstances, if found guilty, the child should not be given harsh treatment without knowing the situation properly. Investigations may reveal the conditions under which the child did commit a mischief. Psychoanalytical study is essential to bring out on the surface the true causes of his anti-social behaviour.

The following are some of the measures which may check delinquency to some extent:

(a) Children's needs, interests and motives of life should be given due weightage by teachers and parents. They need sympathetic treatment for attending to their problems.

(b) Strict treatment and harsh punishment, and closed jails are the last resort for delinquent children. Undue strictness is not a relief but a vigorous reaction and may promote delinquent behaviour.

(c) Parents, teachers and related members of the society should fulfil their responsibilities in the just spirit and with proper devices.

(d) It is very necessary to deal with adults' sexual urge carefully. Undue pressure and checks may further cause delinquent behaviour to continue. Parents should give due responses and maintain a psychological attitude with regard to sex urge.

(e) Home atmosphere should be congenial. Parents should not keep such persons in the family who are likely to have an adverse effect on children's behaviour.

(f) Environmental treatment to check delinquency is done by improving mutual family relations, and relations among members of neighbourhood as well as of the wider social circle.

(g) Physical defects of children may distort the personality, which may give rise to a criminal attitude, sex-related problems, obstructed desires and social disorganization.

(h) This needs no overemphasizing that school has a huge impact on children's personality. Therefore, well-trained teachers should be appointed who devote their energy to understand children individually. School should provide healthy recreational and co-curricular activities. The curriculum should be flexible and the teaching methods should be according to learners' interest, age and mental level. Teachers' behaviour towards students should be democratic, impartial and social.

Juvenile delinquents should be admitted to the 'reformatory school', and serious criminal cases may be kept in juvenile jails where they may be given constructive education and vocational training. The juvenile children can be taught through games, puzzles, paintings, songs and drama to pant up their feelings, emotions, distress, etc. These also may bring into light the children's mental conflicts, reasoning and imagination and provide clues to deal with them for the betterment of their life.

QUESTIONS

Short Answer Type Questions

1. *Define and explain:*
   - (a) Exceptional Children
   - (b) Delinquency
   - (c) Handicapped
   - (d) Mentally Retarded
   - (e) Problems of Handicapped
   - (f) Crippled Children
   - (g) Blind, Deaf and Dumb Children

Average Answer Type Questions

1. Identifying juvenile delinquency.
2. How is delinquency prevented?
3. Write a note on educating the handicapped.
4. Types of handicapped children.
5. What are the measures to check delinquency?

Essay Type Questions

1. Classroom Activities and Handicapped
2. Problems and Role of Teacher in Case of Delinquent Children
3. Role of Teacher and Handicapped Children
4. Role of Teachers and Parents to Deal with Delinquency

References

Allport, G.W., *Personality: A Psychological Interpretation*, Henry Holt, NY, 1937.

Bernard, H.W., *Mental Hygiene for Classroom Teachers*, McGraw-Hill, NY, 1952.

Bigge, M.L. and M.P. Hunt, *Psychological Foundations of Education*, Harper & Row, NY, 1968.

Chaube, S.P., *Abnormal Psychology*, L.N. Agarwal & Sons, Agra, 1986.

Conger, J.J., *Adolescence and Youth*, Harper & Row, NY, 1977.

Cruickshank, W.M. (Ed.), *Psychology of Exceptional Children and Youth*, Prentice-Hall, NY, 1955.

Hadfield, J.A., *Mental Health and Psychoneurosis*, George Allen, London, 1952.

Mathur, S.S., *Educational Psychology*, Vinod Pustak Mandir, Agra, 1981.

Sharma, Yogendra K., *Textbook of Educational Psychology*, Kanishka, New Delhi, 2004.

Symonds, P.M., *The Dynamics of Parent-Child Relationships*, Columbia University, NY, 1949.

16

Creative Children and the Classroom Process for their Growth

Creativity

Some children are exceptional in the classroom by virtue of their being productive because of having certain qualities, which help them in creative thinking. Their qualities are a source of creative production. The thinking leads to new ideas and facilitates formation of new combinations of associative elements.

Out of the many characteristics of creative children, the most important is the fact that they are able to discover new types of associations instead of common and traditional ideas.

E. Paul Torrance defines creativity as the process of sensing gaps of disturbing, missing elements, forming ideas or hypotheses, and communicating the results, possibly modifying and retesting the hypotheses.

Creative children are able to discover new hypotheses. They can re-test the new ideas and can further modifying the process of thinking. The entire process leads to the creation of new principles, methods, pictures, music, poems, etc.

Figure 16.1

Showing Torrence Process of Creativity

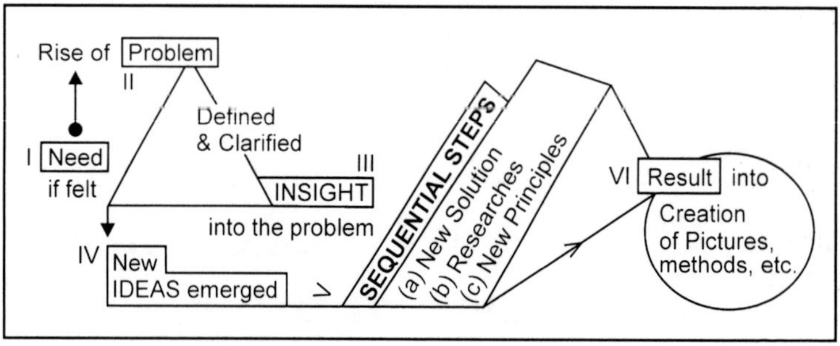

Process of Creativity in the Classroom

The above diagram shows the process of creativity as suggested by Torrence. In the classroom, a teacher introduces the need or goal of the lesson which is to be delivered. The need or significance of the topic gives rise to the problem to be analysed by the teacher and pupils through the content material. Its definition and proper clarification make pupils' understanding elevated, with an insight into the proposition the problem involved. The teacher once again tries to motivate pupils by citing life-related experiences, and also by using illustrations, etc. The process finally gives rise to new ideas about the problem. At this stage, the teacher involves pupils' thinking through interaction and makes substantial use of the new ideas. The interaction gradually passes through new solutions, research and new principles. Finally, new ideas emerge. The teacher now motivates children to make use of new principles and ideas to construct methods, pictures, poems, etc.

The entire process is a novel effort, which is divergent from the common usages. James Drever, therefore, points out its characteristic: "it is the process producing an essentially new product, constructive use of imagination, new combination of ideas or images, self-initiated rather than imitated, synthesis and not a mere summation."

Sir Fedrick defines creativity as bold thinking. By bold thinking, he means divergent thinking, breaking of old norms, having new experiences and creating new combinations.

The process of creativity in the classroom is characterized by a single word: 'divergence'. A teacher can identify a creative child as divergent who is different from others by showing original thinking. It means that in the classroom some children are aware very much of new problems. Their behaviour displays new solutions based on tested experiences and new principles. They show a new approach and dynamic thinking, coupled with original, flexible and novel.

According to the Gestalt theory, the creative process involves thinking, which changes the central point by new organization. It generates insight, which gives rise to ideas different from the prevalent ones. Teachers must try to develop in children the traits of creativity. These include (a) consciousness of the problem, (b) constant understanding for solution by new association of ideas, amicable and also (c) accommodating new and original ones.

The teacher must plan his/her lesson notes which are different from facts given in the textbook. The lesson plan should be based on awareness about the problem, and should be followed by new thinking and new solutions. During the course of presenting

Figure 16.2

Showing Stimuli and Responses in the Classroom

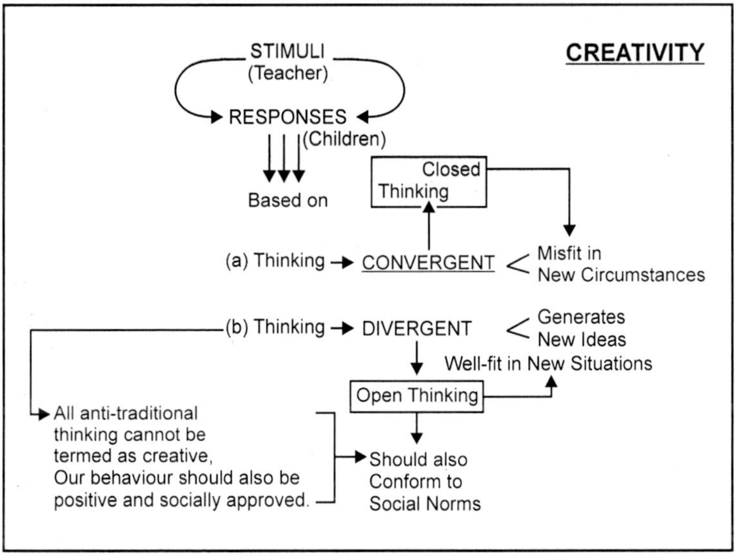

phenomenon, the thinking should be changed according to the new circumstances. The role of the teacher, as is evident, is to develop in pupils the capacity of adjustment through new combinations. The teacher must see that stimuli or problems presented before children generate responses which are different from the convergent ones. The responses should lead to new solutions different from the traditional ones. The traditional solutions cannot be fitted into new circumstances.

Characteristics of Creativity: Teacher Seeks to Develop

Creativity is the process which is based on certain abilities which are to be developed by the teacher. Some of the essentials are given below:

(a) *Awareness of the problem:* The teacher poses problems derived out of the objectives stated in the topic and its introduction. The problems are concrete and generally related with the real experiences of life. The problems generate creative thinking. Therefore, the teacher should make pupils aware of problems. The pupils begin to think about their solutions in ways which are beneficial to make life socially useful and also enjoyable.

(b) *Creative children start thinking in a novel way – divergent thinking:* The problems raised by the teacher may have a number of solutions – some are new and some one old and common. The creative child expresses solutions which are divergent, and may appear awkward. But the divergent solutions are based on dynamic thinking and are novel. The solutions are suitable in the given circumstances. They may be favourable to adjust with the situations. They are also justifiable, being related to social norms.

(c) *Positive result-bound process is creative:* The child who is creative and thinks divergently must also be careful about the end product of the solutions. The result should be useful and may appeal to all concerned, i.e., it should be socially beneficial.

(d) *Creative thinking and behaviour also subject to re-thinking and re-testing:* It can be revised in the present situation. The old solutions cannot be suitable to the changed milieu. The creativity is generally reinforced by the flexibility to accommodate the changing environment wherein the problems take root. The creative person does not hesitate in changing his old and out-of-date views, attitude and behaviour for dealing with problems successfully.

(e) *Creativity is naturally qualified by originality:* The teacher accepts with applause the responses which are original and were not previously expressed. The creative person remains eager to give place to new experiments for inventing original ideas and new methods. His curiosity and keenness to arrive at new things keeps him engaged in investigation and research.

The process of problem-solving in the classroom may develop creativity in pupils through the teacher's initiative. The teacher should state the objectives in terms of socially-approved novel ideas. These can generate divergent thinking and interaction between the teacher and the taught. The teacher's role is to motivate the thinking process by providing life experiences to highlight situations. So long as the problem remains confused, children would go on thinking and rethinking afresh. They would also behave differently and keep themselves re-interpreting the situation and trying tooth and nail to understand the problem.

At the stage of absence of anxiety in children, the teacher must try to understand their half-baked personality. The efforts of the teacher must be to make children neither introvert nor extrovert. Children's personality with their balanced attitude towards problems can bring forth original thinking, unbiased judgment, curiosity and sensitivity. These may develop in children a necessary condition to think anew about problems. A creative person can grasp new ideas and possesses the ability of involvement with the object. The teacher develops in children by motivation the ability to understand the questions involved in the given problem. The teachers make their pupils capable to learn from past failures and reform their thinking by re-testing and re-interpretation.

Traits of Creative Children

In the classroom, creative children show different traits than the normal pupils. These are:

(a) Creative children follow their own path which is novel and detached from the traditional ones.

(b) Their vision is full of insight and is different than average pupils.

(c) Their divergent attitude makes them capable of understanding the problems in their new meanings, fitted well in new situations.

(d) Creative children have the capacity to take risks and follow new formulae. They are bold enough to try again and again and with flexibility. They prefer to follow difficult jobs to reach new solutions, and they enjoy complex aspects of life.

(e) Creative children control their passions, and they are also equally capable of forceful expression passionately.

Promotion of Creativity in Classroom: Nature of Assignments Given for Practice

A teacher explores and provides opportunities to develop creativity among children. They should be given some problems and be asked to point out solutions. A short debate can be organized in the class itself to decide the validity of the suggested solutions. The solutions should be in accordance with the new situations. The teacher should make all efforts to give children constant practice for analysing the problems.

A topic of current situation can be given to the class for discussion. The discussion should be based on information collected by pupils from various sources. Problems from science, geography, art and culture be given to children to probe into their causes and results. A wise teacher may draw the attention of children on current events like strikes in colleges, schools, industries and in various agencies under Local Self Government. Eve-teasing and indiscipline among students bear very intricate problems, and the teacher may invite novel solutions from the pupils. Recently, cases of murder, suicide and ill-fated domestic troubles have been increasing both in rural and urban sectors. These problems may be assigned and the pupils may be asked to hold debates, seminars, essay writing, 'kavi sammelan', etc., under the co-curricular activities. These may increase the capacity of thinking in new perspectives to suggest viable solutions for novel situations. The creative ability of children can be kept alive by such practical exercises.

How is Creativity Improved in the Classroom?

A teacher must be careful about giving due weightage to age and reinforcement to pupils for their critical thinking about a problem. Their divergent attitude and novel suggestions should be welcomed. This type of attitude which is different from the common type of behaviour should be encouraged. The teacher may provide opportunities and help children to be sensitive towards environmental stimuli. They should be taught to test hypothetical ideas and encouraged to use the method to manipulate for solutions to the problems.

Stimulation is also an essential device for developing creativity through new ideas. At the same time, children should also develop tolerance to accept new ideas for solutions to problems. But they should be taught scientifically to analyse the old and set pattern rather than rejecting it forcibly against the new ideas.

It is the responsibility of a teacher to develop a creative classroom atmosphere. Each student should receive with pleasure the various skills and information about the creative process. The teacher can teach ways and means to make full utilization of the available resources for working out ideas. He can provide necessities for self-initiated learning and encourage self-evaluation. Questions in the classroom should be interspersed with intellectual flexibility so that students may become more sensitive. The pupils should be provided with opportunities which are helpful to manipulate situations through materials, ideas, concepts, tools and structures. Creativity can be promoted by encouraging the pupils to consider problems as a whole rather than in the piecemeal.

A teacher should not accept blindly the answers of the pupils and may ask them to reconsider the ideas in terms of the problem. In case of disagreement between two pupils, the teacher may satisfy them by giving clues for re-thinking. At the same time, no comment of a child should be overlooked or missed which might lead to a self-initiated learning opportunity. The teacher's efforts should be directed towards welcoming the learning which is coming from children's interests, motivation and wonderings. He or she should honour the children's own crazy ideas, curiosity and divergent thinking to cultivate a taste for those of others.

Figure 16.3

Classroom Activities are the Product of the Trio Concept of Teacher's Own Skills, Children's Interests and the Problem Solving Devices as Illustrated in the Diagram

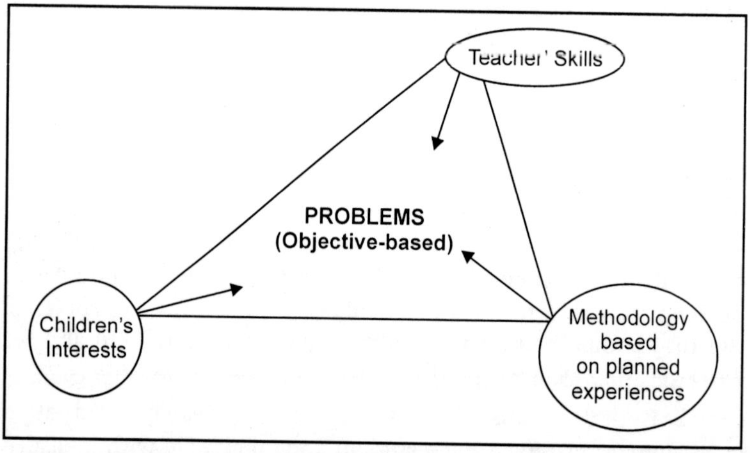

Source: Torrance and Myers – 1970–71, Trio Activities Concept.

Teacher's skills and planned methodology are based on certain principles which are as follows:

1. Recognizing and acknowledging potentialities
2. Being respectful to questions and ideas
3. Asking provocative questions
4. Recognizing and valuing originality
5. Developing the ability to elaborate
6. Unevaluated practice and experimentation
7. Developing creative readers
8. Predicting behaviour
9. Guided planned experiences
10. Searching for the truth with methods of research
11. Creating problem-solving skills.

The above suggested principles are virtually the strategies useful prior to a lesson in the classroom. These principles can help the teacher in improving his performance at every stage, as (a) during the process of a lesson, and finally (b) following a lesson.

The principles of Torrance make the teacher conscious of his responsibilities towards helping pupils with intellectual ability. It requires classroom enrichment, acceleration, and ability. The teacher examines carefully the curriculum and prunes it in terms of goals and interests of pupils. He in the light of the given principles re-examines his teaching methods and selects techniques of teaching in accordance with the revised curriculum.

The teacher encourages his students to use the library exhaustively and engages in experimentation. He directs pupils to have experiences outside the school. The experiences of the wider world of learning make the ground for creativity. The pupils may also be encouraged for writing down their creative ideas. Motivation is very essential to promote and stimulate creativity. Talented students need encouragement to prepare their reports where posters, charts, murals have an adequate scope for promoting awareness of feelings and impressions.

QUESTIONS

Short Answer Type Questions

1. *Define*:
   (a) creative skill
   (b) scientific ability
   (c) torrance process of creativity
   (d) divergent thinking
   (e) environmental stimuli
2. Write briefly about creativity as 'sensing gaps'.
3. Drever's opinion about creativity.
4. Gestalt views about creativity.
5. Creativity and children's task for its successful result.

Average Answer Type Questions

1. Identification of talented and creative students
2. Development of creativity and creative students

3. What are Torrance's principles for teacher's skill?
4. Discuss Torrance process of creativity for classroom teaching.

Essay Type Questions

1. Teacher sought 'characteristics of creativity'?
2. Classroom activities and methods of developing creativity.
3. Traits of creative children.

References

Amidon, E.J. and Others (Eds), *Interaction Analysis: Theory, Research and Application*, Addison Wesley, Massachusetts, 1967.

Barron, F., *Creative Person and Creative Process*, Holt, Rinehart & Winston, NY, 1969.

Bernard, H.W., *Mental Hygiene for Classroom Teachers*, McGraw-Hill, NY, 1952.

——, *Psychology of Learning and Teaching*, McGraw-Hill, NY, 1972.

Bugelski, B.R., *Learning and Motivation*, Henry Holt, NY, 1956.

Chaube, S.P., *Some Foundations and Guidelines for Modern Education*, Ram Prasad & Sons, Agra, 1975.

Dewey, J., *How We Think?*, D.C. Heath, Boston, 1938.

Flanders, N.A., *Some Relationships between Teacher Influence, Pupil Attitudes and Achievement*, Holt, NY, 1964.

Lindgren, H.C., *Educational Psychology in the Classroom*, Wiley International, NY, 1972.

Part V

Classroom, Social Learning and Teacher's Adjustment

17

Teacher, Teaching Practice and Classroom Environment

Who is a Teacher?

Educationally, a teacher means a qualified and trained person who provides instructions to children for improvement of their behaviour in and outside the classroom. Behaviour of each of the school children is based on his or her psychology. Psychology is the study of the behaviour of the individual resulting from his adjustment to the environment. Therefore, a teacher in the classroom is a person who provides instructions to children to mould their behaviour and to make them adjust to the environment in and outside the classroom. The teacher is a psychologist and knows about his pupils' psychology, and accordingly may be able to organize the instructions with the objectives suitable for the modification of their behaviour for the social good.

A teacher is a person who knows classroom children both inwardly and outwardly, their interests, attitude, aptitude and environmental problems. A teacher tries to work for the harmonious development of the behaviour of the child. The teacher in the classroom creates such situations where the behaviour can be developed freely and fully. A teacher is not an unskilled instructor but he is equipped with skills. He knows various means and modes to experiment and organize the class subject matter for the inculcation of awareness in children which can promote capabilities for facing successfully the problems of life.

The motive of a teacher is to bring about such changes in the behaviour of children which are for their good. The teacher must have a good background of psychology because it makes him able to select topics of learning for different levels or stages of children. A psychologically sound teacher can prepare children and make them ready to learn. That teacher possesses the qualities to know his pupils' interests, aptitude and motives. The psychological knowledge of a teacher makes him capable to understand social situations and their proper assessment. Further, the teacher can also evaluate the techniques for the educational growth of learners.

In the end, it is wrong to think that teaching is a very simple affair and aims only to pour information in the child's ears without understanding the pupils' attitude, aptitude and capabilities. Unless you create interest in the learning process, you can never be a successful teacher.

What is Teaching?

Teaching in a classroom is not about telling facts and providing information to children unsystematically. It is not a device to pour into the ears of learners the notes prepared by a teacher out of the textbook.

Classroom teaching is a complex process. The old concept of education is meant to fill the child's mind with stuff to promote knowledge. The child was asked to memorize facts. Therefore, in the past, during the course of teaching, the child's interests and needs were never taken into account. The teaching was merely concerned with providing information or facts about a phenomenon.

The modern concept of education is based on the growth and development of the child at each stage of his life – infancy to adulthood, and even later up to the end of life. It is no more a task involving hard labour to memorize facts and figures. Now, teaching is a joyful process and a child feels happy to learn new things which influence his or her feelings, attitude and capacities. In other words, modern teaching is a process to change the behaviour of children and make them capable of dealing with situations successfully to solve problems.

Modern teaching aims at the harmonious development of the child's personality. The school's environment and teachers in the classroom are there to create such situations where children can develop their personality freely without any force, pressure or mental tension. Now, a teaching job is considered a pleasant affair and a social process for the modification of the behaviour of pupils.

Teaching as a Social Process

The process of teaching, according to H.C. Lindgren, has three focal areas. These are (i) pupils who are learners, (2) methodology which is used to bring changes in the attitude and behaviour of pupils, and (3) the learning situation to facilitate the solution of problems. Each of these focal areas makes the teacher responsible for taking desirable steps for making the pupils adjust with the social environment. The Lindgren trio* is diagrammatically illustrated below:

Figure 17.1

The Lindgren Trio

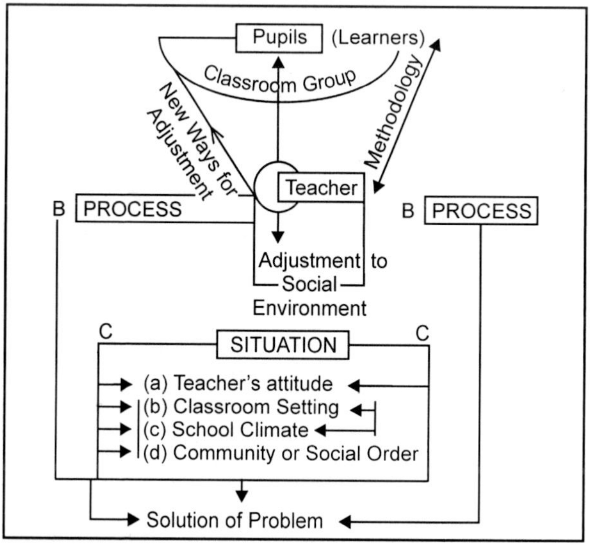

*The Lindgren trio is based on 'Educational Psychology in the Classroom', (Wiley International 1972) pp. 5–7.

Figure 17.1 indicates that the central position in the classroom is occupied by a 'teacher', who is the organizer of the 'teaching process'. The process is a methodology (new order) to change the attitude of 'pupils' for making adjustment with the environmental (social) 'situation'. The situation thus created provides clues to solve the problem in view.

The Pupils (Learners)

Learners occupy the most important place in the trio. Pupils, individually as well as collectively, form a classroom group. The teacher in the classroom is a pivotal point and depends to a great extent on the motives and needs of the pupils. Besides the motives which are correlatives of objectives laid down by the teacher, the teaching process depends on the behavioural attitude in different stages of the learners for effectively harnessing the potentialities of the pupils. Their interests too have to be taken into consideration.

The Teaching Process

The learning process should be organized in such a way that it can influence the pupils' thinking. It is essential that new ways are discovered and utilized which may change the pupils' attitude. Only then can the pupils make adjustments to situations when they behave positively. This can be observed through their activities and also through their way of perceiving and thinking.

The concern of the teacher is to find out what happens when the pupil learns. Why he learns, and what teachers want him to learn or do not want him to learn. This is judged by the ways of adjustment of the pupil towards the situation he or she is facing.

The Learning Situation

What is the learning situation? It is the environment the pupil is facing and in which the process of teaching takes place. The adjustment to the pupil's situation depends very much on the classroom setting, and the community's role in school affairs. These are some of the ingredients of the learning situation. Learning situation must be positive so that it may facilitate a change in the thinking of pupils and also facilitates solutions to problems. By positive situation, the provision of a well-equipped classroom and paraphernalia therein are equally significant, besides the affectionate behaviour of a teacher. The teacher must take into consideration the interests of pupils and be polite and not harsh towards their responses for stimuli. The objective is to facilitate children to make adjustment with the learning situation.

Classroom and Social Situation

Classroom in a school is a primary social situation for a child where he or she comes into contact with various types of children coming from different sectors of social environment. In the classroom, the child gets opportunities to learn the habits, attitude and behaviour of different kinds of individuals or classmates. They interact with each other and their activities become channels of learning and are a key to make changes internally and externally. The classroom develops social behaviour patterns in children and it is the primary place after home where they develop their behaviour. Thus, classroom is considered a ground where children get the atmosphere of democratic situations, i.e., feelings, views and thinking of each other. Here in the classroom, children are introduced to a positive relationship because of the intermixing of various social situations created by the school administration, teacher-taught interaction and behaviour patterns of the pupils.

In the classroom, a social environment is generated, including social forces. The positive mode and successful operation of the various social forces depend on the performances of the classmates. Each child's behavioural pattern – either successful or failure – is noted by the teacher. Thus, in the classroom, children are conscious to perform with care and try to do their work satisfactorily. They also try to keep relations smooth. This process goes on and is the chief means of learning to make adjustment with the social environment.

Group Dynamics and the Classroom

The term 'group dynamics' was coined by Lewin, who proposed that various forces are responsible to architect the behavioural patterns of children in the classroom group. The behaviour patterns of the group promote learning experiences of children in the classroom. Each child is affected and each child affects the group mates, and the teacher takes notes carefully of the resultant characteristics of the group. The teacher takes notice of the changes in the attitude of the child, and after assessing, the teacher tries to bring about the desired changes as per objectives, needs and interests of the children of the group.

In a class of 40 pupils, the teacher may train a small group of four or five pupils. Later, the small group may become the 'peer group'. It plays an effective role in moulding the beliefs, actions and moral behaviour of other students in the class. It is the duty of a teacher to decide when to give group training and when to lay stress on individual training. The group is very helpful and should not be ignored.

Group Behaviour in the Classroom

The teaching in the classroom is done in a group. The group behaviour affects the individuals also. The group characteristics influence the individual child in the classroom. The influence of the group is democratic and the interaction within the group also takes into consideration various social and emotional needs of the individual classmates. The individual pupil in the classroom wants that his social or emotional needs be met. It is only possible when the group teaching is based on a democratic atmosphere. 'All are for one, and one is to follow all'. This may be the ideal of group teaching in the class where the learning will take place in a self-directed and constructive manner. The learning of the child too will be self-initiated rather than depending on others. The teacher must be careful and should take note of the feelings and thoughts of the group or cliques which may cause obstacles in the successful functioning of the learning process. It is also possible that modifications in the behaviour of the children are not desirable, so the teacher may initiate or motivate by providing workable experiences. Under such circumstances, group participation in the light of the solution to the problem is more beneficial. There should be no pressurization.

The role of the teacher in a classroom with a small group is not insignificant. He should play the role of a guide, a leader of the wider social group and of an ideal in the eyes of pupils. He should not hesitate to orient the discussion and to bring them in line by his suggestions or by his experiences. His presence and regular interaction is meant to develop potentialities of the pupils in the classroom. Of course, the teacher for his effective teaching and the role as a leader needs precautions such as:

(a) Alertness towards problems being faced by the pupils.

(b) Consciousness about his position as a leader in the class, and therefore maintaining the needful distance with the pupils.

(c) Cooperate freely with the activities of the group in a democratic manner.

(d) There should not be undue imposition on students; rather, he should be always ready to invite suggestions.

(e) There should not be an authoritative attitude. But, in fact, he is to act ably to develop the traits of a guide in the class to prepare pupils as leaders of tomorrow.

(f) The suggestions should be smooth ones so that the pupils accept these with pleasure.

To sum up, the teacher's job is to seek behavioural changes not of an individual but of the whole group of the class. A skilful teacher facilitates those group activities which develop security and productivity of the pupil. Teacher's constant care and concern is required towards discipline, and he should see that frustration and opposition to change may not crop up in the group. The teacher during the teaching process may encourage group activities rather than textbook contents full of information. Group activities enhance human relations and also promote respect among pupils. Teaching becomes full of joy due to the group behaviour in the social situation of a classroom. The group activities develop certain skills and some of the significant ones are:

(a) Teaching work in the classroom should be a joint venture, and it should be so planned as to involve both the teacher and the taught.

(b) Socio-metric techniques may be utilized to promote knowledge of social relationship among students.

(c) It is essential for joyful teaching to make adequate use of feelings, ideas, and attitude of pupils to handle problems during group interactions. The teacher may suggest projects wherein a group may be involved and the group behaviour is evolved.

(d) Pupils gradually understand the role of leadership in the group when they find their teacher acting like one in the classroom.

The motif is to organize the learning and co-curricular activities in such a way so as to promote success rather than failures. The pupils may learn many things through fair competitions, provided these are organized to suit the group needs and objectives.

Before we close this chapter, it would be fruitful to say something about planning of instructions by the teacher. Intelligent planning begins with the identification of clear and sensible goals. The teacher in planning instructions must keep in mind the following:

(a) Lesson should be based on students' interest.
(b) Arrange the units and material in sequence.
(c) Present new material and avoid the traditional ones based on textbooks.
(d) Planning consists of knowledge as well as its application in day-to-day work.
(e) The teacher must also have contingency plans for remedial teaching for the students who are below average.

QUESTIONS

Short Answer Type Questions

1. *Define:*
   (a) Teacher-pupil, teaching process, pupil's behaviour and teaching goals.
   (b) What is harmonious development of a child?
   (c) Point out and name at least three learning activities.
   (d) What do you mean by classroom environment?
   (e) Distinguish between a problem and social situation.

Average Answer Type Questions

1. Give at least three essential characteristics to plan classroom instructions.
2. Discuss the main skills that a teacher is required to develop through the teaching process.
3. Discuss precautions for the role of a teacher as a leader in the classroom.

Essay Type Questions

1. Teaching process.
2. Classroom environment.
3. Role of a teacher in the changing modern society.

References

Bernard, H.W., *Psychology of Learning and Teaching*, McGraw-Hill, NY, 1972.

Bloom, B.S., *Taxonomy of Educational Objectives*, Longmans, NY, 1965.

Burton, W.H., *The Guidance of Learning Activities*, Appleton-Century, NY, 1952.

Corey, S.M., *Action Research to Improve School Practices*, Columbia University, NY, 1953.

Flanders, N.A., *Some Relationships between Teacher Influence, Pupil Attitudes and Achievement*, Holt, NY, 1964.

Gagne, R.M. and Others, 'Instructional Psychology', *Annual Review of Psychology*, Vol. 20, 1969, pp. 381–418.

18

Classroom Interaction Process

A teacher enters a classroom, delivers a lecture with the help of his prepared lesson plan, and after expressing his ideas, he leaves the classroom after the scheduled period of time. This is no teaching, and this is called a one-sided affair because the teacher delivers his ideas without listening and knowing the reaction of his pupils. He does not interact and has no time to understand the pupils' needs, attitude, capacities and problems. The pupils in the classroom remain silent listeners. This generally happens in today's schools because the aim of teaching is to cover the syllabus and to prepare the pupils to clear the examination. This type of process is called individualistic teaching and is unpsychological.

Interaction: A New Development

A new development in educational research is systematic teaching and the use of classroom interaction. The purpose of interaction in the classroom is to make education a two-way procedure, meaningful and worthwhile.

In the system of classroom interaction, the teacher's job is categorized in a series of levels or stages, i.e., (a) interaction for beginners (b), for average and (c) for mature pupils. The three stages are represented diagrammatically as follows:

Primary Interaction for Beginners

'T' represents teacher and ABCDEFG and H are pupils in the class forming a small group. The interaction is of primary nature to make the concept clear to pupils of normal initial level. The teacher presents a stimulus (problem) and individually pupils in the group respond. The teacher reacts to integrate individually responded versions. The given concept becomes comprehensible to some extent to all pupils of the class.

Figure 18.1

'T' Integrates the Feelings of 8 Pupils

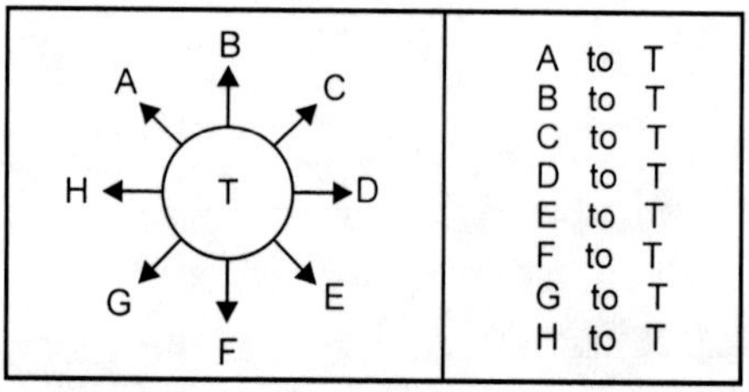

Effective Interaction

The next stage from primary to secondary represents interaction which is more effective than the initial one.

The diagram shows a teacher's interaction with all eight pupils individually and also jointly but in pairs of four. This can be shown as 'T' to A, B, C, D, E, F, G and H and also in pairs of four. A+B to T, C+D to T, E+F to T and G+H to T. Further, four pairs interact with each other, and finally with T.

Figure 18.2

All 8 Pupils Interact Individually and Jointly in Pairs with Teacher

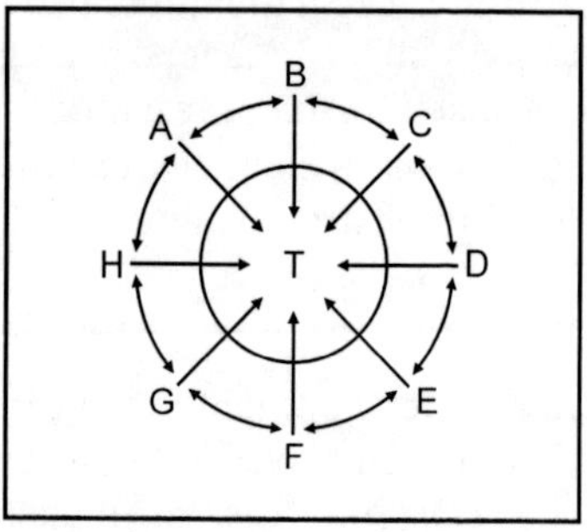

Most Effective Interaction

It is the stage in which primary or immature, average or normal and mature pupils participate and react with the teacher. The teacher's integrative contact influences pupils of the entire (whole) classroom by accepting feelings, encouraging to think further, and to praise for their point of view of significance. The teacher approves and further puts question motivating pupils to solve the given problem.

Figure 18.3

Interaction between Different Groups and Teacher

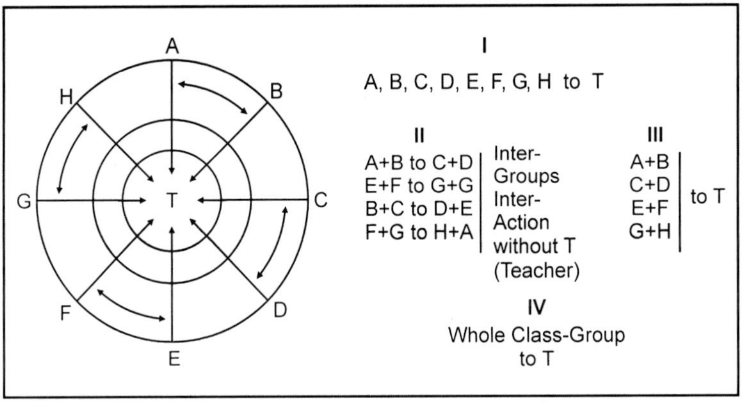

Need for Interaction between Teacher and Pupils

The process of teaching/learning in the classroom involves pupils having their needs and problems, including socio-economic conditions and the environment. In the classroom, an efficient teacher and most knowledgeable pupils face various intricate problems which deserve serious thought and interaction of ideas among themselves and also between the leader of the classroom, i.e., the teacher.

The basis of classroom interaction is research, which according to educationists is the activity meant for the development of behavioural science. The research-based interaction mainly has three aspects: (a) historical, (b) descriptive, and (c) experimental. Historical interaction involves the teacher and pupils to identify the problem, formulation of hypotheses and planning, verification and data analysis. The pupils are prepared and a readiness is developed in them for learning. The interaction is guided by the teacher whereas the pupils get satisfaction to proceed further for the solution.

The next stage of interaction starts with the conditions involved and relationships that exist to solve the problem. Again, the teacher tries to establish adjustment with the situation which is proving to be a hindrance for adjustment or solution.

The experimental stage of interaction is difficult but its consequences are valid and reliable. The experiment is related to the description and analysis of the problem under controlled conditions.

Meaning of Interaction

Classroom interaction is a means to search which is concerned with the practical aspect of the solution to the problem under review. It is more or less based on a systematic approach to solve the problem. It is actually a search that is conducted for the solution of various problems which come across during the day-to-day activities of the pupils, teachers, schools and classroom.

Purpose of Interaction

Purpose of interaction is to promote learning in the classroom. The classroom learning process is different from the learning in a laboratory environment. Interaction between the teacher and pupils in the classroom influences each other. The behaviour of the teacher influences the pupil's behaviour, and at the same time the teacher's behaviour is also influenced by the thinking process of the learners.

Interaction in the classroom should proceed smoothly. If there are interruptions, the pupils may not be influenced to the extent they should be. This may interrupt effective teaching. Effective teaching will only be possible when the interaction takes freely and motives in the minds of pupils and the teacher are clear. The teacher in the classroom must come to know what changes are required in the approach to facilitate the interaction business, and to make it more fruitful.

Interaction Analysis

Quality and effectiveness of the teaching/learning depends upon the quality and nature of interaction. Various aspects of this concept are pointed out below to make the interaction business realistic and most effective.

N.A. Flanders has played a leading role in developing a technique of interaction analysis. Before this, the interactions in the classroom are oral. But later on, through electronic appliances, learning procedures may be observed and recorded. The inferences may be derived and teacher taught behaviour patterns may be known.

Flanders classifies the teacher's role into two broad categories of 'integrative' and 'dominative'.

An Integrative Teacher

Accepts, clarifies, and supports pupils' ideas and feelings, praises, encourages and stimulates students' participation in the decision-making in the classroom.

A Dominative Teacher

Tends to focus on his own ideas and knowledge, gives directions and orders, criticizes students and justifies his own position and authority.

Integrative concept is defined by four categories of teacher behaviour, known as Teacher Talk:

Indirect Influence

(a) Accepts feelings
(b) Praises or encourages
(c) Uses ideas of students
(d) Ask questions

The dominative concept is defined by three categories of teacher behaviour:

Direct Influence

(a) Lecturing
(b) Giving directions
(c) Justifying authority or criticising pupils

The above seven categories deal with the teacher's behaviour.

Student Talk

The Student Talk Response

The teacher encourages students' participation, and welcomes the students' ideas.

Student Initiated Talk

The student talks on his own initiative. After some time, the student may encourage other students to talk, provided the others are willing to talk.

Silence or Confusion

This is a period when no one speaks in the class. There appears confusion.

Method for analysis includes observation and recording in the classroom.

Results

1. Flanders has found that the teachers who used relatively more indirect influences were better able to impress upon the pupils and their teaching was supposed to be successful.
2. The students whose teachers used direct influence were not happy and they considered the process as unsuccessful.
3. Some researchers think that success or failure is not the result of direct or indirect influence. An effective teaching process depends upon teachers who are more liberal and flexible in their teaching process and also in guiding the pupils in the class.
4. The teacher-taught interaction has established that the teacher should always be prepared to accept and encourage the pupils' point of view, feelings and ideas. They can guide pupils better than an authoritative teacher.
5. However, Flanders' technique of interaction is useful in the classroom and should be widely used to assess the problems of teaching in the classroom.

Therefore, the teachers' training process must include Flanders' technique in the curriculum to produce teachers who are effective in helping the pupils learn with pleasure.

In the end, this can be said that Flanders' technique is a valuable tool. It provides an important method for the training of teachers. In our country, Baroda is conducting research to make Flanders' technique more viable in the process of teaching in the classroom.

Below are given some refinements in this technique produced by some of the researchers:

Hough's Category System

Flanders' system refers to teachers' behaviour. M.N. Houghs and her associates developed a method of analysing classroom interaction which also focuses on teachers' behaviour in order to design a means of assessing the quality of teaching. She uses seven broad categories: (a) controlling function, (b) imposition of the teacher, (c) facilitating, (d) developing content, (e) personal response, (f) positive effectivity, and (g) negative effectivity.

The teacher performs his work under the above mentioned domain to influence pupils in the classroom interaction. Hough's system may be used along with Flanders' for leading to a fuller description of teachers' behaviour.

Bellack and Davitz Analysis

They presented another system, concerned with problems of language, whereas Flanders' was based on social psychological terms. Their major assumptions are: (1) verbal interactions among teachers and students, (2) meaning of a word used in the language, and (3) meanings of meaning. They considered the six aspects of meaning as: pedagogical, substantive logical, instructional, instructional (logical) and emotional.

Bellack and Davitz Analysis is based on the fact that in the classroom, the statement either of pupils or of the teacher might convey multiple meanings.

Smith's Cognitive Analysis focuses on analysis of the logical operations. He presents a comprehensive system to describe the logical processes of verbal interaction among speakers. He uses eight basic categories to deal with each specific logical process. The categories included are: (a) defining (b) designating, (c) classifying, (d) comparing-contrasting, (e) conditional inferring, (f) explaining, (f) evaluating, and (h) opening.

Smith's system has an advantage to conceptualize logical teaching.

Gallagher and Aschner's five categories for analysing the interaction stressed on that takes place in the classroom. These include (1) cognitive memory, (2) convergent thinking, (3) evaluative thinking, (4) divergent thinking, and (5) routine.

All the systems as described above are useful. But Flanders' technique of analysis is a valuable research tool and this technique provides a potentially important method for the training of teachers.

QUESTIONS

Short Answer Type Questions

1. What is the need of interaction in the classroom?
2. Define 'interaction between teacher of taught'.
3. Describe the main characteristic of classroom teaching process.
4. What is 'interaction analysis'?
5. Distinguish between an integrative and dominating teacher.

Average Answer Type Questions

1. Discuss categories of integrative concept.
2. Discuss a teachers role as suggested by Flanders' classification.
3. What are 'direct influences' to influence teacher-pupil behaviour in the classroom?

Essay Type Questions

1. Flanders' Interaction Analysis.
2. Seven Categories Dealing with Teacher's Behaviour (Flanders).
3. Classroom Interaction Process.
4. An Improvement on Teaching-Learning Process.

References

Amidon, E.J. and N.A. Flanders, *The Role of the Teacher in the Classroom*, Amidon and Associates, Minneapolis, 1963.

Bellack and Davitz, *Language of the Classroom*, US Office of Education, 1963.

Flanders, N.A., *Teacher Influence, Pupil Attitudes and Achievement*, US Office of Education, Washington, 1995.

Hough, M.N., et al.: *The Assessment of the Quality of Teaching,* Utah University, 1959.

Simpson, R.H., *Improving Teaching Learning Process*, Longmans Green, NY, 1953.

White, W.F., *Psychological Principles Applied to Classroom Teaching*, McGraw-Hill, NY, 1969.

Zahn, R.D., *The Use of Interaction Analysis in Supervising Student Teachers*, Addison Wesley, NY, 1967.

19

Teacher-Pupil Relationship and Adjustment in the Classroom

A pupil in a classroom tries to adjust himself somehow in the environment between the teacher and classmates. Adjustment in the classroom is not an easy process. For a pupil, it requires to strike a balance between the teacher and the situations of the classroom. The situations in the classroom are varied. Lewis M. Terman has done research for understanding how the various forces of a group in the class affect the behaviour patterns or learning experiences of the pupils in the group.

A class may consist of many cliques and to make adjustment among them is a complex affair. A teacher tries his best to stop these cliques from working against the general interest of the whole class. The teacher may provide the required training to the group. The objective is to allow all the pupils to get well adjusted in the process of learning.

The present chapter aims to study the teacher-pupil adjustment with the environment and classroom situation so that a positive relationship between the administration, teacher and the behavioural patterns of the pupils may be created.

Classroom Environment

The classroom has a significant influence on the personality of the child. In the classroom, both the teachers and the classmates mould each pupil's personality by incessant contact through the teaching process and also through co-curricular activities. Teachers in the classroom are ideals and the child pays due respect to them. At the same time, class fellows behave friendly with each other. Children as pupils pass their considerable time in the company of teachers and classmates. The classroom environment, thus, plays a significant role in the formation of the personality of pupils.

Influence of Teacher

Generally, there are two categories of teachers in the classroom. A few are harsh and very strict, while some others behave sympathetically and with affection. The students generally dislike the harsh and strict teachers. Contrary to this, the teachers who are sympathetic are respected by the pupils. This is a fact that the personality of the teacher and his behaviour towards the pupils both exercise an important influence on the pupil's individuality.

Adjustment of Pupils in the Classroom

The adjustment of school children in their classroom is a matter more of the behaviour of the teacher as well as the classmates. The teacher interacts with pupils while teaching in the classroom. This provides an opportunity to children to identify themselves with the teacher. They try to imitate his ways and manners, and personality traits. More important is the fact that if the attitude of the teacher is unfavourable and unmindful of the responses given by a child, the respondent feels discouraged and becomes annoyed while making an adjustment with the classroom teaching.

Teacher talk in the classroom influences pupils' behaviour considerably. It affects both ways – positively and negatively. If the teacher accepts feelings of each pupil and encourages him or her to express themselves, the pupil is motivated to perform better. He feels comfortable in the classroom and also adjustable. The praise of the teacher is just like a capsule for the pupil and he naturally becomes energetic towards the process of teaching. The teacher's role is not just to give direction and authoritative commands without listening to the pupils. This sort of forceful and unconcerned behaviour of the teacher may annoy the pupils. They may feel difficulty in making adjustment with the learning process. Teacher's talk without the cooperation of respondents may create confusion and maladjustment. In this context, Flanders' opinion is fruitful. He opines that in those classes where teachers use more indirect influences, a positive attitude develops and the classroom situations too become amicable to pupils' adjustment.

Co-curricular Activities

Generally the co-curricular activities are performed in collaboration with the classmates. The influences of classmates play a significant role in making the pupils adjust well in the classroom. The classmates get together with a group of their preference, likings and interests. They participate in the activities of their choice. The outlook of the teacher is to seek homogeneity among the participants of the group.

Curriculum and Pupils

The curriculum also has its influence in keeping the pupils engaged and absorbed in the classroom affairs, including teaching. It should not be stereotyped and fixed. A flexible curriculum should be planned which may be according to the needs and current problems of day-to-day life.

Group Behaviour and Adjustment

The classroom environment is affected by the group behaviour and group activities. The teaching process too takes place in a group situation. For pupils, the relationship with a teacher is effective when the process of learning takes the shape of interaction. The progress of students depends much on fulfillment of their emotional needs. The adjustment of a pupil in the class group depends on emotional satisfaction as well as the fulfilment or achievement of the goals of learning. It is, therefore, advisable to foster a two-way relationship, i.e., (i) one-hand interaction in the group, and (ii) the interactions in a teacher-centred class. The individual and social relations both need cohesiveness to make the pupils adjust in the classroom situation.

For adjustment, it is necessary to create in the classroom a democratic atmosphere. It means a situation should be created wherein the pupils take initiative and are self-directed and constructive. The learning process should not take place under pressure. The teacher has to by all means seek unity and avoid situations that generate conflicts and tension. Adjustments in the classroom can be sought by group participation for bringing behavioural and attitudinal changes of the pupils.

Teacher-Pupil Adjustment in the Classroom

Teacher-pupil adjustment in the classroom is a psychological problem. In the classroom, pupils of differing abilities and capacities study together. It is, therefore, a necessity to gauge the abilities of the pupils to make them adjust with the working or teaching process. The teacher, of course, is well versed with the teaching methodology, but at the same time he should be familiar with the pupils. Modern education relies on human psychology and stresses more on the learner than the matter to be taught. The adjustment in the class is based on the goal to develop the personality of the pupils. It is a psychological problem.

Education is not for developing comprehension about a particular phenomenon; it is a process of developing the pupil's mental faculties and abilities. The adjustment in the class demands that the teacher should be aware of different kinds of programmes to satisfy and solve the pupil's life problems.

The teacher is required to plan different courses both for brilliant and also for deficient pupils. The classroom adjustment can only be possible when the pupils get an opportunity of learning multiple aspects, i.e., science, arts, literature, commerce, agriculture and technical. Pupils are eager to learn dramatics, about tourism, leadership, etc., by means of audio-visual aids, television, films, computer, etc. The classroom environment should be organized in a way to make pupils adjust for receiving the instructions joyfully.

Teacher-Pupil Relationship and Classroom Adjustment Demand a Behavioural Laboratory

Modern education in the classroom nowadays needs a laboratory to test the mental capacity and fitness of pupils. There must be some sort of arrangement where a pupil's behaviour is attuned to face and deal with problems. The job of a teacher is not merely to teach cognitively the various subjects of the syllabi. The teacher is supposed to act like a doctor to diagnose the difficulties, mental or social, of pupils and refer accordingly to parents or even to psychologists. A study of psychology is an important part of the teacher-training curriculum. In reality, it is a matter of hard truth that a psychologist has now become an important link for the adjustment of pupils between the home and classroom. The only way for adjustment is to develop behavioural changes in pupils for the individual and social good.

A healthy teacher-pupil relationship makes the classroom adjustment pleasurable with bipolar efforts. The teacher is required to change the traditional methodology and should also equip the classroom. The provision of modern teaching aids includes the use of radio, cinema, cultural programmes, debates, competitions, tours and hikes, visits to historical places and knowledge of heritage games, social service and NCC, students' union and elections, etc. These all have proved amicable both for pupils and teachers to seek fruitful adjustment.

QUESTIONS

Short Answer Type Questions

1. *Define:*
   - (a) Classroom environment
   - (b) Adjustment of pupil
   - (c) Influence of teacher
   - (d) Co-curricular activities
   - (e) Group behaviour

Average Answer Type Questions

1. Discuss teacher-pupil talk and give an example from the subject of school teaching.
2. What do you mean by teacher talk? Give an example.
3. How do curricular activities help in making the pupil adjust in classroom?

4. What is the relationship between curriculum and pupils?
5. Discuss teacher-pupil relations in the classroom.
6. Explain group behaviour and adjustment in the classroom.

Essay Type Questions

1. Teacher-Pupil Relationship in the Classroom.
2. Adjustment of Pupil in the Classroom.
3. Classroom: A Laboratory for Behaviourism.

References

Bigge, M.L. and M.P. Hunt, *Psychological Foundations of Education*, Harper & Row, NY, 1968.

Bruce, W.F. and A.J. Holden, *The Teacher's Personal Development*, Henry Holt, NY, 1957.

Chaube, S.P., *Some Foundations and Guidelines for Modern Education*, Ram Prasad & Sons, Agra, 1975.

Flanders, N.A., *Some Relationships between Teacher Influence, Pupil Attitudes and Achievement*, Holt, NY, 1964.

Gronlund, N.E., *Sociometry in the Classroom*, Harper, NY, 1959.

Terman, Lewis, M., *Genetia Studies of Genius*, Vol. 1 Mental and Physical Traits of a Thousand Gifted Children, Stanford University Press, 1925.

Lindgren, H.C., *Educational Psychology in the Classroom*, Wiley International, NY, 1972.

20

Social Behaviour and Learning

Social Behaviour

Pupil-teacher relationship in school gets several opportunities for effecting a desirable change in the behaviour of students. The school is a fertile ground where several kinds of individuals meet and interact. The interaction among several types of people – students and parents and school authorities – paves the way for learning and, therefore, it is a dynamic process. Social behaviour and learning in the classroom go together, and for this business the classroom becomes a social situation. It is here that a number of activities are performed with the coordination of pupil-teacher and administration of the school. The atmosphere of the school and more particularly of the classroom must be democratic in nature. It generates the tone which is positive and builds a strong relationship between the social environment of the classroom and students.

Social Situation

It is clear that in a school and classroom the process of socialization of pupils take place and social behavioural patterns are developed. The function of a classroom in a school is bipolar. It is the ground where the learning process goes on incessantly, and it is a typical machinery to evolve behavioural patterns of students. The classroom of a school, therefore, is also called a typical place where the social situation is generated by the interaction of a number of social forces. The field of education, as pointed out in modern social psychology and its concept, is the relationship between the teacher and the pupil. This should be understood in the wider context of the social situation. The environment of the class includes many students and teachers. They interact and generate the social situation.

Classroom Social Climate

The classroom is not supposed to be a gathering of pupils and teachers. There are several factors which are responsible for building a social and emotional climate of the classroom. The main factors include: (a) teacher-pupil relationship, (b) social interaction among pupils, (c) the relationship among members of the school staff, and (d) the physical paraphernalia of the classroom.

The social climate of the classroom is bound to affect the behavioural pattern of the pupils. Teachers' cordial relationship or quarrelsome attitude with each other, and their sympathetic or rude behaviour with pupils, their conflicts with the head of the institution, etc., are situations which affect the process of learning. The pupils feel annoyed and discouraged and their tempo of learning becomes low and diffused. The atmosphere of the classroom, or the social situation of the classroom, is greatly responsible for effective learning.

A democratic atmosphere or congenial climate promotes behavioural changes among the pupils for the social good. It is also the source of better behaviour among the pupils and teachers. The classroom atmosphere should not be autocratic. This may create several problems and pupils may become the source of undesirable activities and indiscipline. In a study, Mathur and Bedi have pointed out that there is a high positive relationship between the administrative climate of the school and the behavioural pattern of the students.

Social Group and the Classroom

Social group in the class has various forces which affect the behavioural patterns or learning experiences of the members in the group. The group needs training. The teacher must know after proper investigation what forces are active in the classroom. He has to decide about these forces, the conditions under which they operate, their consequences, and the way these can be modified. Some of the findings indicate their influences on teaching in the classroom. These are:

(a) Pupil's attitude is influenced by the groups of which he is a member. If the attitude requires a change, the teacher must decide when to give individual training or group training to achieve the desired goal successfully.

(b) The small groups are cohesive and are responsible to bring about the behavioural changes. Their control is stronger over its members.

(c) Obstruction from the groups may be removed to allow functioning of learning smoothly.

(d) The cohesive group can achieve its objective easily because of its stronger energy.

(e) A class may consist of many cliques striving for achieving the varied goals. If they are not working for the general good of the class, they should be stopped.

(f) Group training is better than individual training for the performance of social activities, and to bring about behavioural changes.

It is clear that group dynamics influence both the progress in learning and the type of learning. The educational importance of group dynamics is evident from the fact that both the pupil's attitude and behaviour be modified.

Methods of Teaching and Social (Group) Behaviour

M. Terman Lewin, who has worked on social (group) behaviour, opines that a small group of four to five students is very effective in a class of 40. The main aim of teaching in a group is to mould the beliefs, actions and moral behaviour of other students in the class.

'Teach one and teach all' is the motto of group teaching. In group teaching, each individual is influenced. The teacher remains careful to establish a democratic atmosphere and tries his best to develop self-directed and constructive methods. There should be no pressure and no student should be made to feel dependent on any other for meeting his social and emotional needs. Following are the group characteristics which influence individual pupils:

(a) Teacher must take care of interactions taking place among pupils. Teacher may make use of the pupils' interactional situations in his teaching.

(b) The classroom group and the teacher-taught face two types of situation: (i) the individual group member's social emotional needs, and (ii) achievement of the goals of learning. Efficient learning takes place when the individual becomes the member of a team.

(c) The group situations in the classroom affect the learning process. The teacher can stimulate the interaction through special group techniques. The teacher should create a democratic situation.

(d) The teacher should choose his teaching method taking into consideration the cliques, the small groups and other cohesive groups. The teacher is aware of the fact that small groups influence the behaviour of the group members effectively.

(e) The teacher's participation in the groups facilitates modification in the behaviour and attitude of the pupils.

(g) Group psychology can be utilized for problem-solving. It is because of the fact that small groups have more self-confidence than individual members. But it is desirable for problem-solving effectively that a group as a whole participates.

How does group behaviour gel with the teacher? It is made clear by Lewin through the following three stages (Figures 20.1, 20.2 and 20.3).

First Stage

The teacher selects six pupils (A, B, C, D, E and F) and each interacts individually with the teacher as a member of the group.

Second Stage

The interaction takes another turn and three groups of two pupils out of the six, now reinteract with the teacher, and come to a revised conclusion.

Third Stage

The interaction comes to the result by six groups formed inter-individually as shown in the Figure 20.1. Teacher and an individual make a group. Therefore, there is resultant interaction between six groups and teacher.

The net result of the interaction with the teacher sufficiently makes clear the significance of social norms, ideals, moral behaviour as follows:

(i) Varied social customs prevail and affect pupils' learning;

(ii) Bright and dull pupils have their own reasons for different ways of behaviour; and

(iii) Learning has its impact and may change the beliefs which do not suit the present social environment.

It can be summarized that the teacher should also give preference to the feelings and thoughts of the small groups,

Figure 20.1 to 20.3

Interaction of Group with Teacher

I Stage

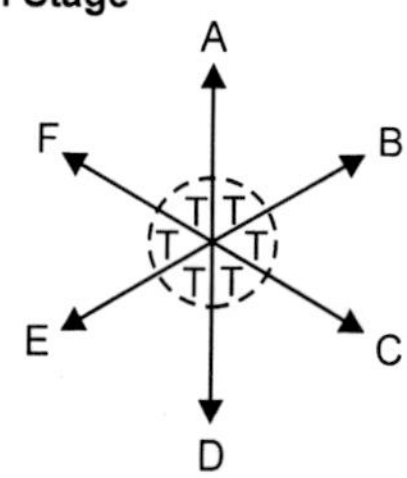

Figure 20.1

(T) Teacher and ABCDEF = Pupils in a Group

II Stage

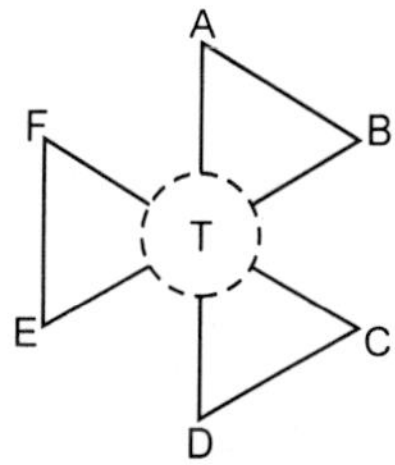

Figure 20.2

I Groups. Each Group has 2 Pupils.

A–B → T
C–D → T
E–F → T

III Stage

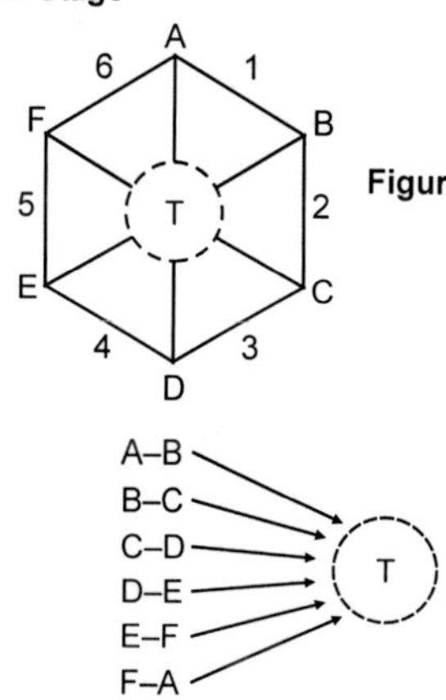

Figure 20.3

but not of the members of the cliques who try to obstruct the process. There may be occasions when some modifications in the behaviour of the individual members are desirable. In such cases, the teacher should encourage group decision.

Out of the class of 30 pupils, there remain 12 pupils who are not the members of groups. But they remain as active 'observers.

Pupils as Observers

In a classroom, some pupils are observers, but they do not learn equally. The observers, who depend upon others, adopt readily the behaviour pattern of their models. Some pupils who are greatly reinforced are more prone to imitate the successful teachers.

Neglected pupils too need the feelings of belongingness or of being loved, and they identify themselves with the teachers and try to imitate their behaviour. The failures try to copy the behaviour of successful models. The teacher should present before them successful models for imitation.

An observer who identifies himself with the characteristics of another person thinks, behaves and feels like his model in a classroom. Both the model and patterns of reinforcement are very significant. In a classroom, one is observing the other and there are many patterns of reinforcement. So, both the model and reinforcement play a major role in learning.

In a classroom where a teacher takes the place of a model, the observer's learning too is influenced greatly. The observer imitates the behaviour of the teacher. Naturally, the teacher controls the behaviour of the pupils. Thus, the teacher becomes a controlling factor of the future course of learning of students. There may be some teachers who do not have a control over pupils, and the future course of the pupils' learning too is different from the behaviour patterns of such teacher. In simplification of the impact of models, it can be concluded that the status of a teacher will serve as a strong influence in shaping the behaviour of students.

Learning in the classroom is both a direct and indirect affair. A pupil identifies himself with the characteristics of another pupil, or a group of pupils. But, a pupil as an observer in the class indirectly observes the behaviour and working of a teacher. The teacher is indifferent of his position as being a model for observers. If the teacher has earned a good name, prestige and success, the behavioural patterns of the observers are influenced by the model teacher. The observer learns many things from the teacher without letting him realize, such as his style of speaking and analysing a phenomenon, his movements in the class, his writing on the blackboard, his aptitude of stating problems and also some of his physical habits and supporting a fact by examples of life experiences, etc.

In a classroom, it is an important part of learning that the teacher's behaviour is imitated greatly but indirectly. The observers learn many things just by sitting, looking and listening in the class. Therefore, it is most essential for a teacher to impress upon the students the learning process, including elements and concepts.

Teacher's Skills for Promoting Learning

Learning and teaching is not an individualized process. It involves group activities. The activities consist of the learner's curriculum, the level of learning stage, and their objectives, including needs and interests. Modern methods of teaching include new skills to solve life-long problems. Simply learning textbook material, lecturing and questioning in the classroom are not enough to enthuse children. Now human relations are too complex to be solved by the passive role of a teacher in the classroom. It is now needful to integrate psychological, sociological and eclectic tendencies to make the process of teaching child-centred. The process of education should be based on individual differences rather than the homogeneous and traditional methodology.

Teaching is not merely the propagation of knowledge. It now aims to integrate knowledge, social situations and the preservation of culture and heritage. Modern curriculum is the integration of science, arts and humanities, including moral, religious and spiritual subjects. It is needful, therefore, to base the method of teaching not only on theoretical instructions but also on extra or co-curricular activities. The process should include, therefore, the stress on the mother tongue. It fosters originality and creativity. The national and international languages may become the study of higher stages.

It is also a matter of serious concern that a classroom, school, management, teachers and the pupils do not cohesively organize the activities. The school activities should be organized in such a way as to encourage responsibilities cohesively, freely, and also with equality and fraternity. The administration should be liberal and democratic. To conclude, a base should be provided to all of them and human relations and group activities should be well knitted.

The teacher must use new skills for class teaching. These include:

(a) Skill in planning the teacher-taught work and involvement of pupils for each to share responsibilities.

(b) Use of projective techniques to foster group interaction.

(c) Teacher should be there to provide effective leadership to groups and also to the entire class.

(d) Teacher must use his caliber for creating a democratic atmosphere through cooperation and also through his independent conduct.

(e) It is the responsibility of a teacher to maintain records of progress of the pupils. The lot of backward students may be given extra guidance to bring them at par with the other students.

(f) Orientation of behaviour, beliefs and ideas should be done by the group method.

Social behaviour and learning is the modern technique and method of teaching. The teaching learning process is based on interactions among the students and teachers. The teacher should take note of the feelings and thoughts of the pupils, and may disallow the cliques who impede the teaching process. The teacher can control the social situation in the class only when he himself functions as a leader. He should maintain his ideal status, position, intelligence and personality in the class, otherwise the cliques may get an opportunity to create indiscipline. The teacher should not hesitate to play the role of leadership, and should also try to develop potentialities of leadership in the students.

A good teacher promotes group activities but for amicable results should see that pupils are self-motivated. All activities of an experienced teacher influence the behaviour of students. The teacher's behaviour essentially comes out through verbal communication with the students. Thus, both the teacher and student influence each other. A good teacher uses various types of activities in the classroom to achieve various aims of teaching.

QUESTIONS TO ANSWER

Short Answer Type Questions

1. *Define:*
   (a) social behaviour
   (b) social situation
   (c) classroom social climate
   (d) social group

Average Answer Type Questions

1. Briefly describe what forces are active to influence pupils' attitude in the classroom
2. What are the methods of teaching used for social (group) behaviour?
3. Discuss the role of pupils as observers in the classroom to achieve the aims of learning.
4. Discuss teacher's skills for promoting learning in the classroom.

Essay Type Questions

1. Social Behaviour and Learning
2. Methods of Teaching Social Behaviour
3. New Skills for Teaching Social Groups

References

Bernard, H.W., *Mental Hygiene for Classroom Teachers*, McGraw-Hill, NY, 1952.

Burton, W.H., *The Guidance of Learning Activities*, Appleton-Century, NY, 1952.

Groulund, N.E., *Sociometry in the Classroom*, Harper, NY, 1959.

Lindgren, H.C., *Educational Psychology in the Classroom*, John Wiley, NY, 1972.

Movis, G., *Practical Guidance Methods for Principals and Teachers*, Harper, NY, 1952.

Simpson, R.H., *Improving Teaching Learning Process*, Longmans, NY, 1953.

Mathur, S.S. and H.S. Bedi, "Impact of Administrative Climate on the General Behaviour Pattern of the Students", *Journal of Education*, Vol. XVIII, No. 2, Punjab University, Chandigarh, 1961.

Thorndike, E.L., *Human Learning*, Appleton-Century, NY, 1931.

21

Teacher's Own Adjustment in Classroom Environment

It is very essential for a teacher to make adjustment with pupils, with the school administration and with the classroom itself for performing his duties as a teacher. It is the quality of a teacher to make adjustment with the various situations in a school to deliver the goods as desired by the society and by the democratic setup of our country.

What do we mean by a 'quality teacher'? A quality teacher is a different personality from an ordinary coach or a guide who is only to make children conscious of the subject matter. A quality teacher has special and high mental abilities and has a knowledge of human psychology to cope with the environment of school and the classroom social situation.

A teacher who has got training in educational psychology can face human problems in and outside the classroom because he understands human nature. The motive of teaching in the classroom is to develop in children social conduct to face the problems of life successfully. Therefore, a teacher who possesses the knowledge of educational psychology can make adequate adjustment with the social environment of a school, and more particularly, with the classroom situations.

Qualities Required for Adjustment

What is required of a teacher to develop qualities for adjustment in the classroom? Some of them are as follows:

(a) For proper adjustment, the teacher has to have a proper attitude to deal with the situations in and outside the classroom.

(b) A sympathetic and unbiased attitude towards learners is essential. It can make a teacher capable to deal with the problems of children who are below normal or very high above normal.

(c) The teacher for proper adjustment in the class must develop in himself the understanding of pupils' behaviour objectively* (see Appendix Tables A-1 and A-2).

(d) The teacher must possess the skills to organize his lessons psychologically. It develops in him the confidence and he can make proper adjustment.

(e) A teacher who possesses an insight and can judge the pupil's mental make-up, is able to adjust in the classroom because he can establish a balance with his pupils.

(f) A teacher who knows well that social relationship is of utmost importance in the process of teaching can make adjustment comfortably.

(g) It is essential for a teacher to develop the skills for organizing activities according to the needs, attitude, and interests of children. The activity-based teaching facilitates the teacher to establish equilibrium with the classroom environment. The students' participation in group activities helps the teacher to make adjustment with any situation in the classroom.

(h) A teacher's job is very complex. He has to develop a good rapport with the pupils, be at ease with the learning process and be comfortable in the classroom physical-social climate.

---

*For the study of pupil's behaviour objectively, the teacher may take help in conducting the survey of his classroom pupils by the two tables given in the Appendix Tables A-1 and A-2.

Besides these, a teacher has also take into consideration the culture and ideals of the institution and the administration. This requires the teacher to develop a scientific attitude and human psychological traits to face varied educational problems.

(i) An experienced and skilled teacher is always prepared to analyse his own and others' behaviour to make adjustments. He must possess a flexible attitude and must allow suggestions and ideas by others who are in any way a part of the classroom environment.

(j) The teacher must have a command over various methods of teaching. He should in practice try to use methods according to the needs, objectives and interests of children. The new methods and technology bring the teacher and the taught closer and adjustment in the classroom is naturally possible.

A prospective teacher essentially needs proper training for adjustment in the classroom. H.N. Rivlin has stressed that a prospective teacher must get special training for facing the new problems and social situations in the classroom. He has pointed out five golden rules for seeking adjustment:

(a) Pupils of various stages, i.e., from infancy to adulthood can be judged in the classroom. Study their needs and interests and understand their behaviour, including attitude and capacities, before teaching them bare facts of phenomena.

(b) A teacher who has a good knowledge of educational psychology can very well understand the personalities of learners. The classroom problems can be solved only through developing an insight for application of the rules of social psychology.

(c) Classroom climate plays an important role for a prospective teacher. It should be favourable, both physically and socially. The climate can foster the ways in which learning takes place.

(d) Adjustment of a prospective teacher depends a lot on his ability to learn and to know pupils inside out. It means the teacher is expected to understand his pupils' interests, attitude, behaviour and habits, etc., as well as the relationship of the outside social environment.

(e) Steps should be taken by the teacher to guide the child suffering from withdrawal tendencies to develop satisfying ways of meeting social situations (see also Appendix Table A-3).

(f) Adjustment of a teacher depends on his continual learning practice. A prospective teacher should keep himself abreast with the application and knowledge of educational research.

Whatever has been discussed above is in favour of some essential skills which are required for a teacher to adjust in the classroom and to be comfortable in the course of the teaching process. In the following paragraphs, the situations responsible for maladjustment are discussed. It is also important to know how a maladjusted teacher can seek adjustment.

Maladjusted Teacher

Who is a maladjusted teacher? One who is anxiety-ridden, nervous, suffering from insomnia and is unable to make adjustments in the classroom is called a maladjusted teacher. A teacher is also called maladjusted who pulls the child by his or her ears, hair, kicks them, mimics them, quarrels with all, etc. If a person shows anti-behaviour normally and suffers from irritability and is immature emotionally, he should be identified as moving gradually towards maladjustment.

A teacher who is usually in the habit of sarcasm in the classroom, and scolding pupils off and on, or he is cruel in punishment is also supposed to be a maladjusted. Some of the teachers habitually pick up quarrels with the staff members, they suffer from insecurity and they feel difficulty in their working because of lack of homogeneity. They are unadjustable in most of the situations in and outside the classroom.

Mental Health and Maladjustment of a Teacher

If the mental health of a teacher is not in proper order, the teacher cannot feel adjusted in the class and remains uncomfortable. This is because of a common understanding that the teaching profession is considered of the lowest degree in India. The common notion is that one who is not successful in getting a job of his choice at last prefers to enter the education sector as a teacher. He is not mentally satisfied with the teaching profession and remains upset. Teaching is not their first choice, and they have no interest and love for teaching. They cannot do justice with their pupils and remain maladjusted. Mentally, they suffer from insomnia and are considered maladjusted.

The teachers of private schools get very low remuneration for their job in India. They, therefore, are not committed enough for their profession and show an attitude of not being concerned. In private aided schools, the teachers remain frustrated because there is no security of job. They feel that their service can be terminated any time without notice. The pressure of teaching too is immense and they are required to teach more than 40 periods (each of 45 minutes) a week. In this situation, they are not expected to do justice, and consequently it results in the poor performance and lack of mental equilibrium among the teachers.

The pressure of administration and the undue harassment by inspectors and supervisors keep the teachers mentally upset.

The social conditions of teachers, the family environment, and status and prestige among the people in the city or village are deplorable. This naturally affects their mental health.

Finally, Mathur* concludes that the main causes of frustrations, mental conflicts, etc., which affect the mental health of a teacher can be summed up as: inadequate salaries, no interest in teaching and allied work, no security of tenure, authoritative management and supervision, poor conditions of family and above all, restrictions on their personal activities.

Reformation for Better Adjustment in the Classroom

A maladjusted teacher can be made to adjust provided some of the discrepancies are tackled and the teachers feel that their profession is noble. There should not be any ignominy about the profession of teaching in the minds of teachers themselves.

The adjustment in the classroom demands commitment for the job of teaching. It the teachers do their job well, they would be respected by the students, and also by the people outside the school. Generally, the society has a favourable opinion about teachers and has feelings of sympathy, affection and love. The teachers are considered as a peace-loving community. But some of

*S.S. Mathur, "Administrative Policies Governing Substitute Teachers Serving in Higher Secondary Schools in Major Cities of U.P.", unpublished Ph.D. thesis, Agra.

the teachers themselves by their negative approach have damaged their image. Some teachers have become selfish and have started private tuition shops. They have lost their prestige. Being money-minded and accepting work for tuition and coaching is not noble for the teaching community. It is necessary that a feeling of confidence should be developed for one to get respect in the classroom.

Adaptation to Classroom Environment

A teacher who is mentally unhealthy struggles for adjustment in the classroom. Adaptation leads to working peacefully in the classroom, whereas maladjustment leads to decay and frustration. Thus, the teacher has to develop traits of adaptation. Education makes the way clear for adapting to the classroom climate. The teacher of educational psychology learns to inculcate good habits to modify the odd situations of the classroom. These may be cliques of children who obstruct the way of learning. A teacher for making adjustment first tries to overcome diversities of religion, race, castes, languages and attitude towards life. These may improve the classroom environment.

The teacher must develop in him the type of behaviour the society expects from him. He should deal with his pupils in an ideal manner. This may help him to adjust in the classroom. The teacher's own behaviour is the index for the children to imitate. The authorities of the school should not hesitate in providing amenities for the teacher in the classroom. It is essential that the teacher is allotted a classroom where normal facilities for teaching are present. For example, the classroom should be well ventilated and there must be proper arrangement for natural light, fresh air and sufficiently comfortable seating arrangement according to the number of pupils in the class. The blackboard, lecture stand, demonstration table, and facilities for operating electronic devices like overhead projection, filmstrips, slides, etc., are essential for teaching through modern technical methods. These make the teacher satisfied with his profession, and he tries to do justice. The teacher too feels satisfied in his position and also adjusts with ease.

The teacher in the classroom cannot feel at peace if he picks up quarrels with the children or with the principal or with any authority appointed to look after his work. It is generally found that authorities do not produce chargesheets against a teacher without sufficient causes. For the adjustment, it is better to settle the issues through amicable meetings. The teacher, if he is committed to his work and sees that his activities are according to the principles of education, will not face any problem in his adjustment in the classroom.

Maladjusted teachers pollute the classroom climate and have no respect in the eyes of children. Rude behaviour towards children and harsh punishment create disrespect for teachers, which is difficult for making adjustments. The only way out is to mould his own behaviour to regain the respect of children. A balanced way of thinking and carrying on with the job committedly may make the teacher get adjusted once again and he may feel healthy mentally to shoulder responsibilities.

QUESTIONS

Short Answer Type Questions

1. *Define:*
   (a) classroom adjustment
   (b) teacher's mental abilities
   (c) qualities for adjustment
   (d) behaviour of teacher
   (e) pupil's attitude
   (f) adaptation

Average Answer Type Questions

1. What are the causes of a teacher's maladjustment in the classroom?
2. Who is called a maladjusted teacher?
3. Discuss the main characteristics of an adjusted teacher.
4. What are the five rules of adjustment?
5. Discuss the relationship between mental health and classroom adjustment.

Essay Type Questions

1. Maladjusted teacher.
2. Qualities required for a teacher to adjust in a classroom.

References

Bernard, H.W., *Mental Hygiene for Classroom Teachers*, McGraw-Hill, NY, 1952.

Crow, L.D. and A. Crow, *Mental Hygiene*, McGraw-Hill, NY, 1951.

Hadfield, J.A., *Mental Health and Psychoneurosis*, George Allen, NY, 1952.

Lindgren, H.C., *Educational Psychology in the Classroom*, Wiley International, NY, 1972.

Glossary

Aims of Teaching: To assist in defining and setting up educational objectives in terms of desirable behaviour.

Aptitude: It means those symptoms which tell the amount of efficiency with which a person may learn things to face a situation or a problem.

Backward Child: A backward child in a class is unable to do the normal work and his performance normally is below average for his age. He or she is also considered as a problem in the class.

Binet-Simon Scale: The tests are arranged in age groups to formulate the idea of mental age. Thee are certain activities that an average child of a given age can perform successfully so that any individual can be said to have the mental age corresponding to the problems that he can solve.

Child-centred Education: Everything in education, the methods, the process, the curriculum, etc., should be adopted to the psychological tendencies of the child.

Classroom Social Situation: In the classroom, children get opportunities to mix up with each other, and they learn the habits, attitude and tone of behaviour of different kinds of individuals or classmates. In the classroom, there is generated a social environment, including social forces. It is the ground where democratic norms develop due to the behavioural patterns of children coming from different sectors of society.

Convergent Thinking: It refers to thoughtful processes with integrative and distinctive structural frameworks.

Creativity and Creative Children: Creativity is the process of sensing gaps of disturbing, missing elements, forming ideas or hypotheses. Creative children are able to discover new hypotheses. They can re-test the new ideas and can further modify the process of thinking.

Delinquent Children: Delinquent children are those who deviate from the norms and ideals of society. They behave against the social norms to the extent of becoming the subject of official action.

Democratic Atmosphere: In the classroom, democratic atmosphere can be motivated by teachers to train pupils for taking initiative and to become self-directed and constructive. The process should not take place under pressure. Unity is sought in the group and conflicts are avoided.

Development: Development is the product of the interaction of the organism and its environment. It is the process resulting from a constant interchange of energies within an organism and energies within its environment.

Divergent Thinking: It refers to cognitive processes that presumably involve initiative, spontaneity, originality, flexibility, etc.

Educational Psychology: It is an applied branch of psychology studying human behaviour in relation to education.

Exceptional Children: They are of high quality who deviate from the normal in mental, physical and social characteristics.

Flanders' Categories of Interaction: These mainly include 'Teacher talk', 'Student talk' and 'Silence.'

Gifted or Talented: The class of children who performs above average (with IQ above 140) is known as the class of talent.

Group Dynamics: The behavioural patterns of the group promote learning experiences of children in the classroom. Each child in the group is affected, and each child affects the group-mates. The teacher takes notice of the changes in the attitude of the child and tries to bring about the changes as desired by the objectives, needs and interests of the children in the group.

Handicapped: They are children who are physically abnormal and suffer from impairment, inhibiting from participating in normal activities.

Innate Powers of Child: The child's mind has three kinds of innate powers: (a) Mneme, (b) Horme, and (c) Cohesion

(a) Mneme is the result of collection of impressions received by the child's mind. It functions in the child during pregnancy. Therefore, a pregnant mother is often advised to think and behave in a decorous manner.

(b) Horme is the power of purposive activity. Whenever a child acts, it is with some set purpose. Every human activity is purposive.

(c) Cohesion lends order, coherence and system to one's thoughts and impressions.

Integrative Teacher and Dominative Teacher: The teacher's role during interaction can be classified as 'integrative' and 'dominative'. An integrative teacher accepts the feelings and ideas of pupils, while the dominative teacher tends to focus on his own ideas and knowledge.

Intellectual Development and Piaget: It means growth of understanding, memory, imagination, reasoning and intelligence in pupils. Piaget suggests four stages of development as schemes, assimilation, accommodation and equilibration. Children should be taught those things which they can experience through their sensory organs. Concrete operational thinking begins later on, and during the period of mature growth intelligence, children are in a position to understand abstract ideas and concepts.

Intelligence: It is process to generate properties in pupils which make their behaviour positive so as to act better in a novel situation.

Interaction: It is a new development in educational research. A teacher classifies it initially for beginners, then for the average and at last for mature pupils. The process of interaction is a means to search for the practical aspects of the problem.

Maladjusted Teacher: A maladjusted teacher is one who is anxiety-ridden, nervous, suffering from insomnia and is unable to make adjustment in the classroom. He generally beats up children severely for no reason. He quarrels with all and his general frustration comes out.

Mentally Retarded Children: They are children who possess low intelligence and are found psychologically disturbed. They are unable to correlate various experiences to solve the problem.

New Type Tests' Questions: In the new type tests, questions should be so included as to permit all types of children, bright and average, to score in them. Questions should range from extremely difficult to easy ones.

Planning of Instructions: Intelligent planning begins with the identification of clear and lively goals based on pupils' interests. Teaching material is arranged sequentially. Textbook material is avoided and new material is presented through teacher-pupil interaction. The plan should also include a contingency plan for remedial teaching.

Reinforcement Pattern of Behaviour: Rewards and immediate praise of students' performance have a great influence on the learning of the child. The students' behaviour may not simply be controlled by logical content and lesson plans.

Scope of Educational Psychology: It studies three different aspects, i.e., students, process of learning and conditions of learning

Social climate in the School: Social climate in the school and the classroom has three broad categories: (i) autocratic, i.e., where teachers believe in strict discipline, and they treat children with harsh and cruel attitude; (ii) submissive, i.e. where teachers are unable to maintain proper control in the class, children become over-assertive and there is total disorder in the class, and (iii) neither autocratic, nor-submissive, i.e., where climate is usually of comradeship. The teacher and pupils work together.

The Intelligence Quotient (IQ): It represents the degree of brightness possessed by an individual. It is obtained by dividing the mental age by the chronological age.

$$\left[IQ = \frac{M.A.}{C.A.}\right]$$

To drop a decimal point, IQ is multiplied by 100. Thus,

$$IQ = \frac{M.A.}{C.A.} \times 100$$

The Learner or Pupil: The learner or child is the first concern of the teacher. He must understand how the child's mind works before teaching the subject matter.

The Learning Process: It is also related with the psychology of the learner. It is through the learning process that the teacher changes the child's behaviour, attitudes and personality for the social good.

The Learning Situation: It includes the school, classroom environment, various types of learners in the classroom, the objectives to be achieved by the teacher and the expectations of parents and guardians.

Appendices

Appendix I

Table A-1

The 10 traits that are serious for the child and most troublesome for teachers

Rank Order	*Serious for the Child*	*Troublesome for Teachers*
1	Steading	Interrupting
2	Untruthfulness	Carelessness in work
3	Unreliableness	Inattentive
4	Cruelty and bullying	Restlessness
5	Cheating	Silliness, over-smartness, etc.
6	Heterosexual activity	Whispering
7	Impertinence	Tattling
8	Impudence	Thoughtfulness
9	Selfishness	Disorderliness
10	Laziness	Inquisitiveness

Table A-2

Behaviour problems to discharge tension by pupils in the classroom

Physical attacks on classmates
Destruction of school/classroom property
Verbal attacks/swearing/threatening
Combativeness
Symbolic aggression
Blaming one's difficulties on others
Defacing property of school/classroom
Negativism, arguing meaninglessly

Table A-3

Child's behaviour showing withdrawal tendencies and discipline problems

Factors Responsible	*In pre-adolescent stage %*	*Adolescent stage %*
Poor work habits	52.2	51.9
Nail-biting	8.6	10.8
Lack of self-confidence	8.6	13.4
Nervousness	18.6	19.5
Social immaturity	5.9	7.8
Anti-social behaviour	27.4	27.7
Attention-getting devices	16.9	19.0

Survey: N.I.E. (1980).

Table A-4

Exceptional children's (5–19 years) approximate number in school population

Category	*No. per 1,000 pupils*
Mentally gifted	20
Mentally retarded	20
Physically defective	59
Blind and partially seeing	2
Deaf and hard of hearing	15
Crippled	10
Low vitality (delicate)	15
Speech defective	15
Emotionally disturbed	25

Appendix II

Following are some of the experimental assignments which may be assigned to the pupils individually as well as in group of four-five pupils. The pupils may be asked to perform and plan or construct during the practice of teaching; and finally they may be examined by an external examiner.

For Trainees in the Teachers' Training Colleges

1. Draft a plan showing the arrangement of classroom space (draw a plan map).
2. Interact during an interview with a group of five pupils and ask to chalk out a typical set of classroom rules facilitating a congenial environment for learning. (In a group, pupils from various grades should be included).
3. Draft an outline for assessment of behaviour – (cognitive as well as social) – of pupils of the age group 11–18 years.
4. Draft an agenda for a parent-teacher meeting.
6. Suggest steps that a teacher should use to diffuse the problems created by mischievous students disrupting the teaching process.
7. Teacher should allot each pupil a specific topic (based on syllabus) and ask him to prepare a table showing (i) general and (ii) specific objectives for the given topic.
8. Trainees may be asked to prepare a lesson plan as an outline on the schemes of Herbart and Bloom's classifications.
9. Draft a scheme to solve the given problem on Piaget's technique. (Teacher will allot each pupil a problem).
10. Pupils may be asked to prepare a chart showing the seriated process of learning giving an appropriate diagram.
11. Pupils may be asked to outline an 'introduction' for a given topic and the motivation may also be suggested, if required to introduce the topic.
12. Each student may be given a separate topic to prepare a chart on the Bloom's Taxonomy.

[Each pupil-teacher will prepare a 'portfolio' containing at least six assignments as given above. He or she will be examined through a viva-voce by the external examiner.]

Index